Plate 8
Embroidered casket panel
depicting 'Touch'
English, mid-17th century
15.2 x 15.2 cm
V&A: Circ.466–1925

Plate 9
Possibly Miss Bluitt, later
Mrs Payne
Embroidered casket
English, before 1665
29.7 x 26.5 x 18.5 cm
©Ashmolean Museum

Plate 10
Richard Shorleyker
Border designs from
A Schole-house for the Needle
London, 1632
Wood engraving, 14.5 x 18.8 cm
V&A: 95.O.50

Opposite
Plate 11
Matthias Mignerak
Border designs
Paris, 1605
Wood engraving, 18.1 x 14.7 cm
V&A: E.2277–1931

Pattern books often incorporated combinations of different textile techniques; the author might encourage the use of a variety of skills in the foreword or preface. Adrian Poyntz, for example, states in his *New and Singular patterns and works of Linnen* (1591) that his square designs were intended to be multi-purpose: 'it is to be understood that these squares serve not only for cut-workes, but alsoe for all other manner of sewing or stitching.'[11] Similarly, Richard Shorleyker encourages the application of different techniques to the designs. In his preface to *A Schole-house for the Needle* he gives the customer choice in the use of the patterns:

for the disposing of them into forme and order of workes, that I have left to your own skils and understandings; whose ingenius, & well practised wits, will so readily,

(I doubt not) compose them into such beautiful formes, as will be able to give content, both to the workers, and wearers of them…

Shorleyker also provides a grid to facilitate the enlargement or reduction of patterns (pl.12).[12] In a surviving copy of his pattern book in private ownership, two of the borders copied from Mignerak are pricked, possibly for embroidery.[13]

Pricking and pouncing

In his *First Book of Embroidery* (Venice, 1527) Alessandro Paganino (*fl*.1509–38) explains the method of transferring designs to a plain textile for embroidery by pricking and pouncing, a method that has survived with adaptations to this day.[14] He describes how the design is transferred on to tracing paper and pricked along its lines.

The tracing is then pinned to the textile and a bag containing 'pounce', fine powder such as ground cuttlebone and charcoal, is rubbed over the holes. The design is thus transferred to the textile in the form of dotted lines. The textile is stretched over a frame and the pounced lines are painted over, ready for embroidery. One of Paganino's composite woodcut plates (pl.13) shows the design being traced out (bottom right) and a woman rubbing a bag of pounce through pricked lines on to a stretched textile (bottom left). The same plate also illustrates the pounced design being reinforced with paint (top right): the textile is stretched over an embroidery frame set up against a window so that the light shining through the pricked holes will show up the faint lines. The final picture in this plate (top left) shows the embroiderer at work, the textile on the frame now secured in a horizontal position.

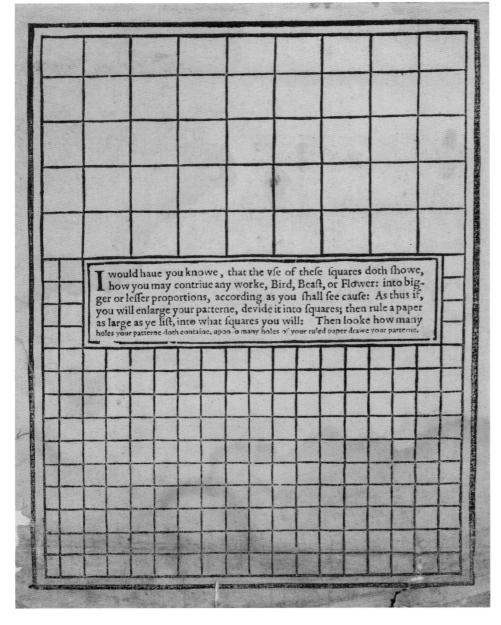

I would haue you knowe, that the vfe of thefe fquares doth fhowe, how you may contriue any worke, Bird, Beaft, or Flower: into bigger or leffer proportions, according as you fhall fee caufe: As thus if, you will enlarge your patterne, deuide it into fquares; then rule a paper as large as ye lift, into what fquares you will: Then looke how many holes your patterne doth containe, upon fo many holes of your ruled paper drawe your patterne.

Plate 12
Richard Shorleyker
Grid from *A Schole-house for the Needle*
London, 1632
Wood engraving,
14.5 x 18.8 cm
V&A: 95.O.50

Opposite
Plate 13
Alessandro Paganino
First Book of Embroidery
Originally printed in
Venice, 1597
Facsimile, 12.9 x 10.3 cm
V&A: 43.A.53

E auertisse con el disegno insieme ti apportiamo vn porsilo bellissi
mo e vago a locchio cosa non mancho da tenerse cara che esso di
segno: laquale cosa da noi sono stata con grandissima fatica com
posta e ordinata a tua vtilita e pochissima spesa.　　Uale.

Evidence of pricking and pouncing can be seen in Rosina Fürst's pattern book, where the reverse of a carnation design reveals that it has been pricked for transfer to a textile (pls 14,15).[15] The V&A collection has numerous other examples of pricked designs, most of which have also been pounced.

While the principle of this method continued over hundreds of years, by the twentieth century pricking was no longer necessarily done by hand: a photograph of the 'drawing room' at the embroidery design company Vicars & Poirson, London (pl.16) shows a perforation machine in use in the 1920s. The pricked design was placed on the textile, then pounced with blue powder and set by spraying with methylated spirits. The finished piece of fabric bearing its blue design was then sold as part of an embroidery kit. One of the designers in the Vicars & Poirson photograph (far left) is Francis Johnston (1889–1965), who worked for the company from 1904 until 1962. One of his designs, for an embroidered table runner embellished with anemones (pl.17), was sold in an embroidery kit; a finished version of the runner is in the V&A collection (pl.18).

Plate 14
Rosina Fürst
Design from *Pattern Book third part*
Nuremberg, 1676
Engraving, 14 x 16.2 cm
V&A: 95.O.16

Plate 15
Rosina Fürst
Reverse of design from *Pattern Book third part*
Reverse of engraving, 1676
Nuremberg
14 x 16.2 cm
V&A: 95.O.16

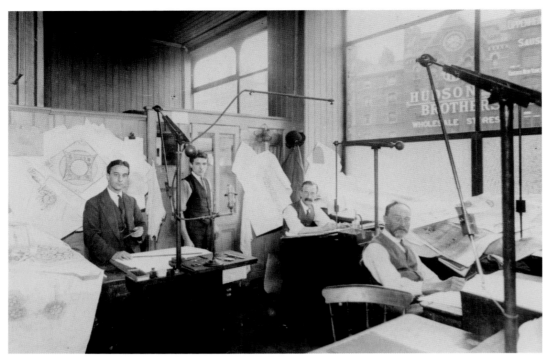

Plate 16
Francis Johnston in the 'drawing room' at Vicars & Poirson, London
1920s
Photograph, 10.1 x 15.2 cm
V&A: AAD/2001/1/1
Given by Kenneth A. Johnston

Plate 17
Francis Johnston
Design for a table runner
1930–50
Coloured wax crayons on tracing paper, 37.9 x 45.3 cm
V&A: E.1556–2001
Given by Kenneth A. Johnston

Plate 18
Francis Johnston
Table runner
1930–50
Embroidery in rayon and cotton
threads on poplin, 99 x 26.2 cm
V&A: AAD/2001/1/1
Given by Kenneth A. Johnston

Iron-on transfers

The beginning of the twentieth century also saw the introduction of iron-on transfer designs for embroidery, which made the process of copying a paper design on to fabric very much easier. The V&A collection has a number of these, of which the earliest pieces were printed by Liberty & Co. in about 1905–9. The continuing commercialization of home-making culture saw the proliferation of iron-on embroidery transfers from the 1920s on (pl.19).[16] These were often provided as 'give aways' in magazines such as *Needlewoman and Needlecraft* and *Good Needlework* (1964–6), of which there are examples in the Ramah Judah and Ephemera collections in the AAD and others in the NAL.[17]

Plate 19
Iron-on transfer from *Good Needlework Magazine*
January 1936
Transfer print, 22.9 x 28 cm
V&A: AAD/3/55/1990
Given by Tim Judah

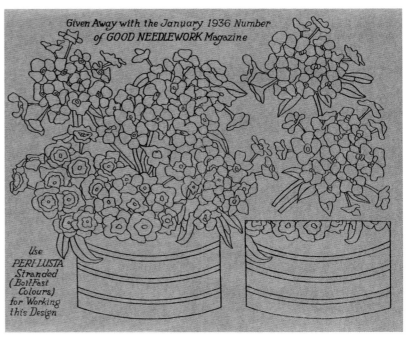

Designers and clients

Ever since the sixteenth century, embroidery designers have tended to work in a wide range of other media – indeed, for many, embroidery design was ancillary to their main career. For example, in the sixteenth century Thomas Geminus (c.1500–1562) and the heraldry designer Johann Siebmacher created designs for goldsmiths' work as well as embroidery. In the seventeenth and eighteenth centuries Daniel Marot (c.1661–c.1745), architect and designer to William III; Amalia Beer (1688–1723), painter and embroiderer; and painter and designer Jean-Baptiste Pillement (1727–1809) all designed for embroidery and other media.

Although born in Lyon, Pillement worked in many European countries before arriving in London in 1754. He returned to Paris in 1767, where his *Work of Jean Pillement* was published by Charles Leviez. This publication, which was used by practitioners in a range of applied arts, established Pillement's reputation;[18] his designs, which he continued to publish extensively, were widely used for embroidery (pls 20, 21).[19]

The seventeenth-century French royal embroiderer Pierre Vallet (1575–c.1642) published engravings of flowers for embroidery, tapestry, painting and manuscript illumination. His publication *Le Jardin du Roy Très Chrestien, Loys [sic]* ..., illustrating flowers from the French royal gardens of Louis XIII, was published in Paris in 1624.[20] Vallet's text includes descriptions of the colours of each flower and recipes for mixing them.[21]

Unlike Pillement's versatile designs, those by Mary Ann Hutton (1819–1901) are for specific items of dress and accessories, such as cap backs, collars, cravat ends, lappets, cuffs, bags and slippers, and for lace, whitework and other embroidery techniques. The earliest designs associated with Hutton, dating to the early 1820s, were probably inherited from her mother, an amateur embroiderer.[22] Mary Ann Hutton was listed in directories as 'dressmaker' in Torquay between 1856 and 1897;[23] many of her designs are much earlier, made between 1839 and 1852. There are over 429 designs associated with Hutton in the V&A, including 237 printed examples, mainly for embroidery, and a large number of drawn and copied sheets.[24]

The growing popularity of embroidered gowns in fashionable circles in England during the nineteenth century ensured custom for the increasing number of dressmakers and milliners in provincial towns, with some of the better-known practitioners supplying manufacturers in towns and cities in other parts of the country. In Bath the number of dressmakers and milliners grew from 141 in 1824 to 379 in 1866–7;[25] ten embroiderers were recorded in the city in 1864–5.[26] Inscriptions on some of Mary Ann Hutton's designs indicate that she sent lace and embroidery to Bath, possibly under some kind of subcontract. Close commercial links between Hutton in Torquay and a Mrs Scott are indicated by inscriptions 'Honiton lace Mrs Scott' and 'Front of Honiton Habit Shirt Mrs Scott' on designs. Mrs Scott was probably Mrs Sarah Scott, a dressmaker known to have been working in Bath in 1865–6.[27] Hutton's widower father, recorded as a commercial traveller in 1870, was living with his daughter at the same address in Torquay by 1862; it is likely that Mr Hutton was by this time transporting goods for his daughter's dressmaking business.[28]

Titles and dedications in printed pattern books produced by professional embroidery designers of an earlier period, dating from the sixteenth to eighteenth centuries, reveal that their designs were intended mainly for female, amateur embroiderers.[29] Some European design books of the sixteenth, seventeenth and eighteenth centuries included a moralizing foreword extolling the virtues of embroidery as part of general housekeeping, listing technical instructions or opining about women's intellectual abilities.

The foreword to Margaretha Helm's (1659–1742) *Further Delights* of 1742 demonstrates how embroidery pattern books contributed to the public discourse about the abilities and capabilities of women.[30] Helm argues that the craft of embroidery, far from subjugating women, should be one of a range of activities, including intellectual pursuits, in which they should participate.[31]

Many of these pattern books also had a dedication to female – and occasionally male – members of wealthy or noble families, no doubt as a marketing strategy. Embroidery was considered an essential accomplishment for young girls and married women from well-heeled families,[32] with finished pieces being mounted on to objects such as caskets or looking-glass frames, used to cover cushions or made into bookbindings for bibles and prayer books.

Examples in the V&A include caskets and samplers with embroidered names and dates, objects that have survived over the centuries, steeped in the history of the families from which they came and passed down through the generations as heirlooms, often in the female line.[33]

Even after the introduction of printing, pattern books with drawn rather than printed designs and a manuscript dedication were made for an elite minority.[34] The Venetian designers Lunardo Fero (fl.1559) and Amadio Novello (fl.1559) each produced hand-drawn pattern books containing almost identical designs, but with small variations, such as a change to one motif or its colours, enlargement or reduction of a design, or the suggestion of a repeat without depicting it fully (pls 22, 23). Their dedications are almost word for word the same, Fero's to Elena Foscara and Novello's to Barbara Molin.[35] The last design in each volume represents the family coat of arms of the recipient, with the same framing device but in different colours. Clearly either both designers worked from a single source, or one of the designers was copying the other.[36]

Two copies of a seventeenth-century German pattern book made for three intermarried families, the von Wimpffen, von Kressensstein, and Schlüsselfelder, contain a dedication and coats of arms of the three families.[37] Among the few surviving English pattern books, one rare example contains an introductory poem mentioning the names of royalty – Mary I, Elizabeth I and Mary, Queen of Scots – and members of the nobility, the Countess of Pembroke and Lady Elizabeth Dormer. As a rule, however, English pattern books tend to be aimed at a broader clientele.[38]

An engraving by Abraham Bosse (c.1602–1676) of about 1635 depicts a fashionably dressed woman embroidering flowers including a tulip on a piece of fabric in her lap (pl.24).[39] Realistic flowers such as this were first published in 1606 by Pierre Vallet, embroiderer to the King Louis XIII of France. Similar patterns were made by designers employed in the French silk weaving industry who were members of the exclusive silk-weaving guild known as La Grande Fabrique, in Lyon. Those in the V&A are part of a huge collection originating in the workshops of La Grand Fabrique that has been dispersed to other parts of France, to Britain, Ireland, and across the Atlantic.[40]

Plate 20
Jean-Baptiste Pillement
Design for engraving,
published in *Collection of
various Fantastic Flowers* …
Paris, *c*.1760
Black chalk on paper,
17.2 x 27.7 cm
V&A: E.286–2011

Plate 21
Waistcoat (detail)
1785–1800
Embroidery on silk
6.3 x 23.7 cm
V&A: 170–1898

Overleaf
Plate 22
Lunardo Fero
Page from pattern book
Venice, 1559
Pen, ink and watercolour,
19.3 x 14.5 cm
V&A: E.1940.17–1909

Plate 23
Amadio Novello
Page from pattern book
Venice, 1559
Pen, ink and watercolour,
22.3 x 16.2 cm
V&A: D.1751.11–1908

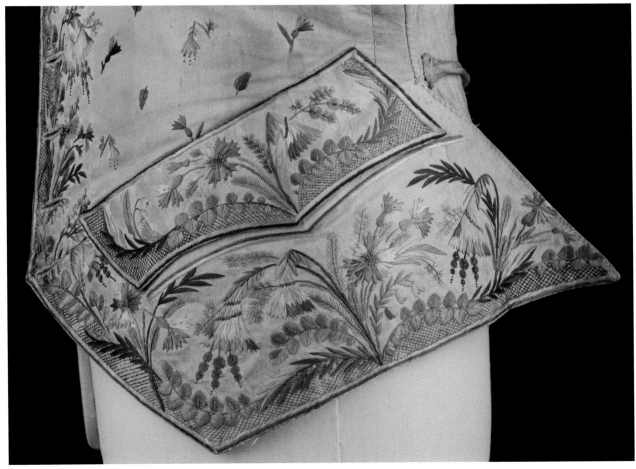

Presentation designs shown to particular clients, perhaps as examples from which to choose, would not have been widely shared, and thus retained their exclusiveness. Examples in the V&A collection include eighteenth-century French patterns for waistcoats and male suiting, mainly for embroidery in coloured silks on silk, and designs for hems and sprigs for women's gowns. The Museum holds more than 90 of these, the earliest being a waistcoat embroidery design of the 1720s to 1730s (pl.57), the majority of the rest dating from around 1780–90.[41]

The practice of creating presentation designs to generate business for embroidery designers developed in the seventeenth century, a fine example being the trade card of 1690 of Parisian embroiderer Jean Magoulet (*fl*.1690).[42] During the eighteenth century fashion retailers employed professional designers and embroiderers in considerable numbers to meet the demands of a growing market, providing fashionable embroidery to be included in garments of all kinds, for both men and women.[43] By the second half of the century and into the nineteenth, printed designs were being made available to amateur embroiderers in magazines and periodicals such as *The Lady's Magazine* (1770–1832), *The Lady's Newspaper* (1847–63), *The Englishwoman's Domestic Magazine* (1852–79) and *The Queen* (1861–1970).

In the nineteenth and twentieth centuries embroidery was designed by an eclectic range of artists and craftsmen – as in previous centuries – as well as specialists in embroidery. Examples include the Pre-Raphaelite artist Edward Burne-Jones (1833–98), whose designs were characterized by accurate observation and vivid colour;[44] the great designer, craftsman and manufacturer William Morris (1834–96), who was also a writer and revolutionary socialist; illustrator and painter Walter Crane (1845–1915), also a prolific and versatile designer;[45] and the painter, Arts and Crafts bookbinder, jeweller, embroiderer and illuminator Phoebe Traquair (1852–1936).[46] More recently, artist and designer Julie Verhoeven has worked in art direction in both the fashion and music industries.

Plate 24
Abraham Bosse
Woman embroidering
c.1635
Engraving, cropped to 31.2 x 22.3 cm
V&A: E.6052–1911

Plate 25 Valance
Italian, 16th century
Embroidered silk velvet,
31 x 278.5 cm
V&A: 37–1903

Designing for embroidery

The development of design for embroidery evolved over time to meet changing taste in furnishing and fashion fabrics, sometimes requiring the dimensions of a pattern to be altered to fit the shape of the object. The process of accurate adaptation required a grid, such as that published by Richard Shorleyker in *A Schole-house for the Needle* (pl.12). At other times, particularly in the case of embroidered furnishings and decorative objects with simple shapes, designs could be transferred with very little adaptation. For example, the popular seventeenth-century motif of a lady fishing in a pastoral setting appears on a printed lining paper in the V&A collection (pl.26), with dimensions almost identical to an embroidered casket panel now in Glasgow (pl.27).

By contrast, designs for embroidery in fashion needed to be flexible and versatile and were often required to fit a particular shape on a section of fabric. For example, embroidered borders, insertions or appliqué sections might require a repeating pattern (pls 25, 38);

designs might have to fit horizontal collars or vertical bibs (pl.106), braces, clocks (a type of stocking decoration) and lappets (pl.106); and waistcoats, horse trappings and saddlecloths (pls 81, 82) demanded that embroidered decoration fit neatly into meticulously measured asymmetrical pieces. Embroidery design also had to allow for changing weights of materials, as can be seen in some eighteenth-century designs where codes are used to indicate particular types and techniques of metal threadwork. Heavier embroidery would be best supported where fabric could be folded under and stitched down along hems and centre-front openings or in double thicknesses on pocket flaps and plackets, while skeletal embroidery designs were required for lightweight chain stitch with drawn threadwork on light fabrics such as muslin (in the eighteenth century) or organza (in the twentieth).

Embroidery is particularly well suited to decoration of items of clothing, since it can allow a higher degree of pictorial detail and

variety of colour and texture than weaving the design into the fabric. Eighteenth-century designs for woven, brocaded silk waistcoats and coats often have details that resemble embroidery on or around the pocket flap, hem and centre-front opening (pl.32). However, these designs are limited by the technique of brocade weaving, where the motif is made by the pattern weft, which is supplementary to the ground weave and only taken across the width of the motif.[47]

From the 1780s to the early nineteenth century, the borders of men's suits in France were sometimes decorated with *broderie en rapport*, pieces worked separately on small embroidery frames and sewn together to complete the finished garment. In his *The Art of the Embroiderer* (Paris 1770), embroiderer and printer Charles Germain de Saint-Aubin (1721–86) describes the use of the *dessin marqué*, the design marked with instructions given to embroiderers to ensure that they were all working from the same design. The complete repeat

Plate 26
Lining paper
English, late 17th century
Woodblock print, 39.5 x 49.5 cm
V&A: E.405–1968
Croft Lyons bequest

Plate 27
Embroidered panel
English, mid-17th century
39.5 x 51 cm
CSG CIC Glasgow Museums
Collection

Plate 28
Margaretha Helm
Design from *Further Delights…*
Nuremberg, *c*.1742
Engraving, 38.8 x 28.5 cm
V&A: E.1147–1933

Plate 29
Wallpaper
English, late 17th century
Woodblock print, 54 x 48 cm
V&A: E.1003–1976
Given by Boots the Chemist, Kingston
upon Thames, Surrey

Plate 30
Coupon
Lyon, *c.*1785
Bodycolour, 24.1 x 14.6 cm
V&A: E.203–1930

Plate 31
Bord for a *veste* pocket
Lyon, *c.*1785
Bodycolour, 15.6 x 28.9 cm
V&A: E.257–1937

Mr Huddleston & Crofts. Capt Lekeux March 3. 174⅔

Plate 32
Anna Maria Garthwaite
Design for a woven silk coat
1743
Graphite, watercolour and lead
white on paper, 46.4 x 26.7 cm
V&A: T.391–1971

Plate 33
Veste
French, 1780s–90s
Embroidered silk, 63.5 x 33 cm
V&A: T.231A–1917

Plate 34
Coupon for a *veste* or *gilet*
Lyon, *c.*1785
Bodycolour on tracing
paper, 20.7 x 13.2 cm
V&A: E.274–1937

of a design, usually 7–8 in (18–20 cm) long and beginning and ending at the same place in the design, was known as a *coupon*. These repeats would be joined to complete a border.[48] The *coupons* in the V&A are on oiled paper used as tracing paper; these were once transparent but have now browned with age;[49] on some the white bodycolour traced outline is still visible. After a design had been traced onto the *coupon* the copy was finished with bodycolour to indicate the distribution of light and shade (pl.34).

Similarly, in the nineteenth century designers of embroidery patterns might also provide instructive annotations. Among the designs by Mary Ann Hutton is a drawing of about 1848 with instructions in her own hand: 'centre of pines & leaves Green Terry, edged with gold twist; tendrils gold twist; – pines with a row of dotting between the gold twist. – worked on Maroon Velvet'. The same design, turned through 45 degrees, appears on another sheet as a lithograph rather than a drawing.[50] This suggests that the drawing was traced from the lithograph and the instructions copied by hand so that two people could use the same embroidery pattern simultaneously, in order to increase

Plate 35
Mary Ann Hutton
Designs for chemisettes
1856–97
Pen and ink, 42.4 x 28 cm
V&A: D:1242–1901

the speed of production. In 1881, at the age of 62, Hutton is recorded as having Blanche Hosking, assistant dressmaker, aged 29, living in her household.[51]

The arrangement of many patterns in multiple orientations on the same sheet of paper appears to be an embroidery design practice that endured from the eighteenth century until as late as the 1960s (pls 35 & 145).

Design sources and techniques

Floral motifs have dominated embroidery design since the Middle Ages. Prints in herbals (books illustrating plants and their habitats for identification and medical purposes) were a rich source of inspiration for embroidery in the sixteenth and seventeenth centuries. Images of plants in early herbals were frequently distorted or adapted for practical reasons, such as fitting the shape of a plant into a printing block or illustrating several phases of a plant's life – bud, flower and fruit.

These pragmatic decisions reappear in designs such as Matthias Mignerak's pattern book of 1605, where, for example, leaves and nuts of a tree appear the same width as the trunk.[52] Similarly, Mignerak's pomegranate tree (pl.36) bears both buds and fruit, following a principle established by botanist Leonhart Fuchs (1501–66) in his *De Historia Stirpium*, published in 1542.[53]

Sprigs from pea and strawberry plants arranged into borders for embroidery in gold, silk or crewel in Richard Shorleyker's *A Schole-house for the Needle* (1632; pl.38),[54] as well as spot motifs and floral slips, can be traced back to a succession of botanical sources, such as Walter Dight (*fl.*1588–1619), Thomas Trevilian (b. *c.*1548) and the early sixteenth-century Helmingham herbal and bestiary. Dight employed Shorleyker as an apprentice and left him the business when he died in 1619.[55] Shorleyker registered *A Schole-house for the Needle* with the Stationers' Company in 1627, along with other titles 'which were Walter Dights [*sic*] his Masters'.[56] Opinion is divided on whether Trevilian copied or initiated the embroidery designs in his manuscript volumes: *Miscellany*, dated 1608, held in the Folger Shakespeare Library in Washington, DC, and *Great Book* of 1616 now in the Wormsley Library, Buckinghamshire. But the similarity between his drawings and the stylized plants in the earlier Helmingham herbal and bestiary is unmistakable.[57]

In the eighteenth century, with

Plate 36
Matthias Mignerak
Fruit tree design from *The Practice of the Industrious Needle*
Paris, 1605
Wood engraving, 18.4 x 14.8 cm
V&A: E.2245–1931

Opposite
Plate 37
Valance
English, 1650–75
Embroidered silk satin, 233 x 79.5 cm
V&A: T.322–1980
Given by Miss Margaret Simeon

Plate 38
Richard Shorleyker
Design from *A Schole-house for the Needle*
London, 1632
Wood engraving, 13 x 16.9 cm
V&A: 95.O.50

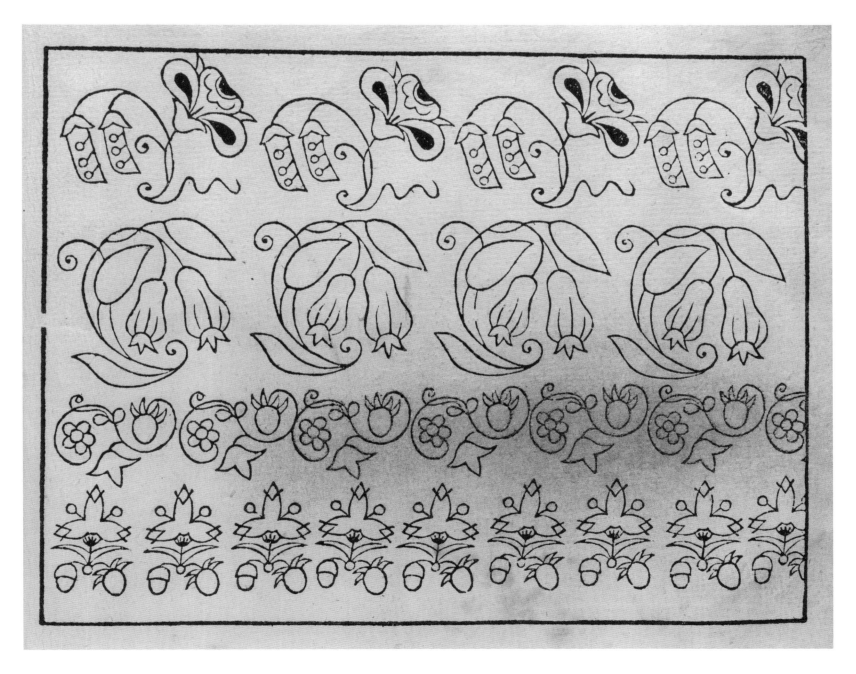

designing for the French silk industry in mind, training in flower drawing was offered from 1760 onwards at the free drawing school in Lyon, the Ecole royale gratuite de dessin.[58] Among the many pencil and watercolour studies produced by designers are some finely detailed watercolours of plants now in the collection of the Musée des Tissus in Lyon (pl.39).[59] Mastery of botanical drawing enabled designers to create floral fantasies for woven and embroidered silks, such as a design for the edges of the centre-front opening and hem of an embroidered waistcoat of about 1785, now in the V&A collection (pl.40). These flowers also show the influence of the great French designer Jean-Baptiste Pillement.[60]

Plate 39
Vetch
Lyon, 1760–85
Watercolour, 8.8 x 8.8 cm
Musée des Tissus: Musée des Arts Décoratifs de Lyon

Plate 40
Bord for a *gilet*
Lyon, *c.*1785
Bodycolour, 18.7 x 24.1 cm
V&A: E.247–1937

Opposite
Plate 41
Carl F.W. Wicht
Design for a lambrequin
Berlin, 1850–60
Bodycolour, 20.7 x 34.7 cm
V&A: E.2028–1935

Plate 42
William Morris
Design for a wall-hanging, *c.*1878
Watercolour on calico, 139.7 x 109.2 cm
V&A: E.55–1940

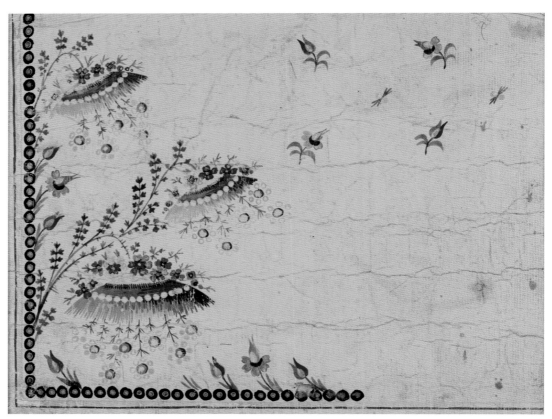

Berlin woolwork

The V&A collection includes numerous designs for Berlin woolwork, a technique that became popular in Britain from the 1830s and typically includes brightly coloured stylized flowers combined with classical decorative motifs.[61] Originally printed in Berlin as early as 1804 on a grid of squares to represent the threads of the canvas, the patterns were then hand-painted in bodycolour (if not printed in colour) to indicate the colours of the dyed wools to be used for embroidery. Carl Wicht's design for a woolwork lambrequin, an ornamental hanging covering the edge of a shelf or the upper part of a window or door, is a dazzling array of jewel-like colours (pl.41). Most of the main and some lesser-known Berlin and Paris manufactories are represented in the V&A collection. There are also a number of loose patterns published in French and British magazines.[62]

Morris & Co.

One of the great strengths of the collection is the holding of drawn and painted embroidery designs by William Morris and his daughter, May (1862–1938); these reveal a strong reaction against the conventions of Berlin woolwork design. This is demonstrated by the fluid lines and balanced colours of William Morris's design for an embroidered wall-hanging of about 1878 (pl.42) for Morris & Co. The V&A textile collection includes versions of the finished panel in two colourways, one of them possibly embroidered by May Morris (pl.43). A considerable collection of further embroidery patterns produced by Morris & Co. Art Workers Ltd between about 1880 and 1939 resides in the V&A.

The twentieth century

The birth of the Arts and Crafts Movement at the end of the nineteenth century brought with it a new enthusiasm for embroidery design. Examples include embroidery patterns for furnishings by designers such as Phoebe Traquair, who became one of Scotland's leading Arts and Crafts artists. Some of Traquair's designs show the influence of the great Arts and Crafts artist Walter Crane: her drawing for the border of a work bag (pl.45), for example, has strong echoes of a series of designs by Walter Crane commissioned after 1875 to help improve the standard of design at the Royal School of Needlework (pl.44).[63]

Some 60 years later, the Needlework Development Scheme was established in Scotland in 1934 with the parallel aims of encouraging embroidery and raising the standard of design in Britain. This collaborative project between art and design education and industry continued until 1961; a number of embroidery designs for the scheme are in the V&A collection.

Also among the twentieth-century embroidery designs in the V&A collection are 187 Russian designs and floral designs from Paris of about 1900, such as that on an embroidered floral mantle by the couture house Worth, made in 1909 under the head designer, Jean-Philippe Worth (1856–1926).[64] Embroidery continued to play an important part in French couture of the 1920s, '30s and '40s – with evidence of the influence of the imported styles such as the japonisme and orientalism popularized by the Ballets Russes in 1909.

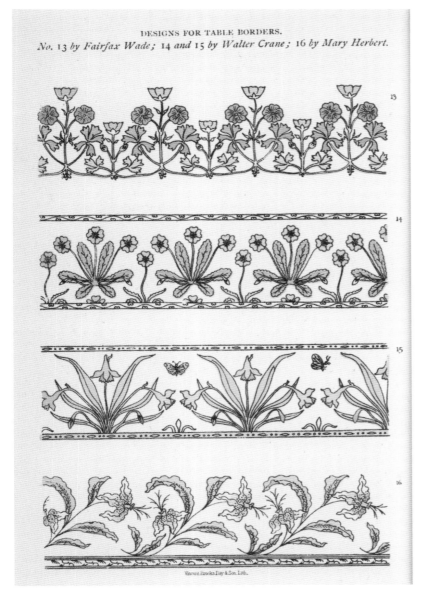

Opposite
Plate 43
May Morris (?)
Embroidered wall-hanging, *c.*1880–95
Silks, 248.8 x 200.6 cm
V&A: T.66–1939

Left
Plate 44
Walter Crane
Designs for table borders From Letitia Higgin, Royal School of Needlework, *Handbook of Embroidery*, London, 1880
Colour lithograph, 21 x 13 cm
V&A: 43.D.38

Above
Plate 45
Phoebe Traquair
Design for a work bag, 1880–95
Graphite and coloured pencils on paper, 8 x 26 cm
V&A: E.1021–1976

FASHION

FASHION

Stem patterns

Botanical patterns dominate the field of
embroidery design, providing the widest
possible range of shapes and colours, the
use of curling leaves and stems offering
limitless flexibility to the designer seeking
to fit embellishment to garment shape.

A mid-sixteenth-century Italian design
in *New Work* (Venice 1543), a pattern book
by Domenico da Sera, uses a combination
of curled elements and intricately wound
branching stems of columbine to fill the
field of a wide border pattern (pl.46). The
design, 7 cm wide and with a pattern repeat
of 19 cm, would have been suitable for
a cuff without the need for reduction or
enlargement. This motif was widely used:
a similar ornament is embroidered in blue
silk cross stitch on the neck piece and cuff
frills of a boy's linen shirt, made in England
at the same period (pl.47).[1]

Plate 46
Domenico da Sera
Design from *New Work*
Venice, 1543
Engraving, 6.9 x 18.8 cm
V&A: 95.L.28

Opposite
Plate 47
Shirt (detail)
English, *c.*1540
Embroidered linen, 89.8 x 70.5 cm
V&A: T.112–1972

Flower embroidery

By the mid-seventeenth century floral designs had become luxuriantly naturalistic, with intertwined stems, leaves and tendrils often filling every corner of a garment. Stimulated by popular interest in botany and horticulture, embroidery depicting identifiable flowers frequently appeared on dress for both women and men. Many of these designs were based on botanical illustrations that were also intended for embroidery, such as those in the *florilegia* of Pierre Vallet (Paris 1624; pl.51) and Guillaume Toulouze's *Book of Flowers* (Montpellier 1656; pl.52), and became fashionable for embroidered gowns across Europe from the early eighteenth century. These designs were contained in pattern books such as Amalia Beer's *Respectable … Delightful Women, in which is contained a … Sewing and Embroidery Book …* (Nuremberg 1715–23; pl.48).[2] Her design for a floral stomacher, a v-shaped panel of fabric to be inserted into an open bodice to cover the front of the corset, includes flowers depicted naturalistically amongst scrolling acanthus in the Rococo style; the design is captioned 'one more to embroider and needle paint'.[3] Beer's flowers are intended to be embroidered in satin stitch and long-and-short stitch, while the scrolls are hatched to indicate that they are to be worked in silver or gold threads.[4]

Following such a design, an English mantua (a type of open gown) of the 1740s in the V&A collection is lavishly decorated with colourful embroidery of naturalistic flowers with contrasting leaves and motifs in metal threads (pl.50).

By the 1840s, bright floral patterns embroidered on a dark background appeared on women's aprons, bags, and shawls, and were echoed in men's waistcoats (pl.49).[5]

Plate 48
Amalia Beer
Design from *Respectable … Delightful Women…*
Nuremberg, 1715–23
Engraving on paper, 30.9 x 40.6 cm
V&A: E.777–1912

Plate 49
Waistcoat (detail)
English, 1850s
Embroidered silk, 56.5 x 29.2 cm
V&A: T.1071–1913

Plate 50
Mantua (with detail)
English, 1740–45
Embroidered silk, 170 x 180 cm
V&A: T.260 & A–1969

Iris Tuberosa

Iris Susiana Maior

Plate 51
Pierre Vallet
'Iris' from *Le Jardin du Roy*
Paris, 1624
Engraving, 30.6 x 17.2 cm
V&A: II.RC.F.9

Plate 52
Guillaume Toulouze
'Rose' from *Book of Flowers*
Montpellier, 1656
Engraving, 18.4 x 13.9 cm
V&A: E.1720–1913

16

Rosa pallida.

G. toulouze. inuen. et. excu. cum. priuil. Regis

Men's dress

In French embroidery of the late eighteenth century, natural motifs were popular decoration for men's dress.[6] A prominent designer of *vestes* and pictorial *gilets* – waistcoats with and without skirts – of this period was Pierre Ranson (*fl.*1750–99), whose work was engraved by Jacques Juillet (b.1739) in *Nouveaux Cahiers de Vestes et Gillets* (*Suite of New Collection of Vestes and Gilets*) published in Paris, around 1773 (pl.54).[7] His stylized roses, in particular, appear in an embroidered eighteenth-century French waistcoat in the V&A collection (pl.53).

Plate 53
Gilet (detail)
French, 1790–1800
Embroidered silk, placket: 4.1 x 16.7 cm
V&A: T.212–1972
Given by Welch Margetson

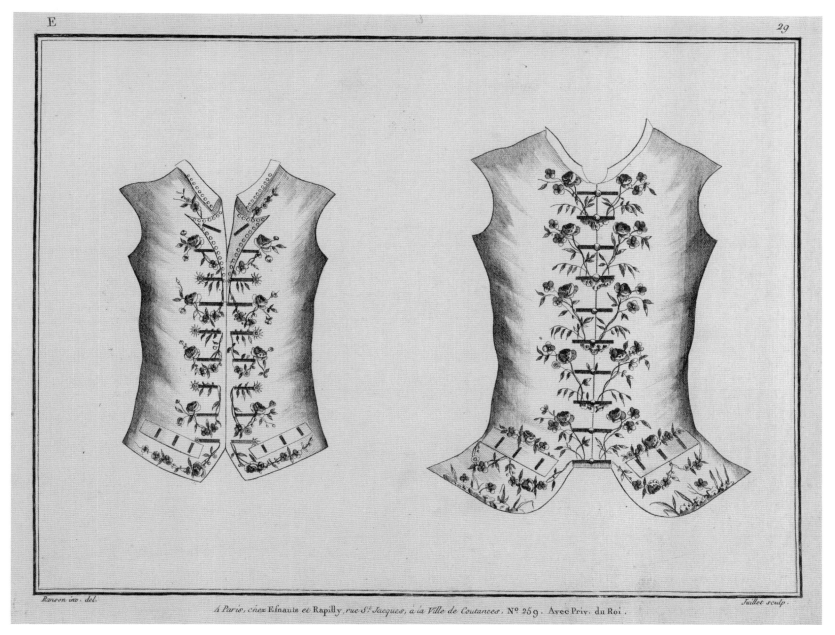

Ranson inv. del.

A Paris, chez Esnauts et Rapilly, rue S.t Jacques, à la Ville de Coutances. N.o 259. Avec Priv. du Roi.

Juillet sculp.

Plate 54
Jacques Juillet after Pierre Ranson
Design from *Nouveaux Cahiers de Vestes et Gillets*
Paris, *c.*1773
Engraving, 23 x 29.7 cm
V&A: E.1372–1906

Metal thread embroidery

Rich embroidery in metal thread was particularly popular in northern Europe in the early eighteenth century. An example in the V&A from this period is a presentation design or *bord* for a waistcoat bearing an inscription: '… satin stitch along the seams — plain *veste*, ornamented with embroidered trimmings, the sum of 2,000 [*livres*], a third off for cash' (pl.56).[8] The *bord* is actual size, to show the client how the trimming would appear on the completed garment. The high price – about £97 in the eighteenth century[9] – confirms that the embroidery was intended to be worked in silver or gold thread. The design includes three stitching techniques: the repeating pattern of foliage surmounted by a flower has rows of short, dark parallel lines indicating double stitches, probably for *gaufrure* (waffle-pattern embroidery); the areas resembling dotted fish scales are for stitched rows of spangles; and the three-dimensional pattern of striped steps inside a curled leaf indicate bands of *filé* (plain) and *frisé* (frosted) gold or silver strips.

Charles Germain de Saint-Aubin was among many subsequent designers to use the same conventions in their pattern books: in his *The Art of the Embroiderer* (1770), published some 40 years later (pl.55), he used the 'fish scales' and contrasting bands in striped steps in his pattern for embroidered ribbons and foliage respectively.

Unmade pieces of fabric intended as parts of a finished garment reveal that pieces were embroidered separately, before being sewn together. A beautifully decorated panel for a waistcoat in the Musée de la Mode, Paris, with intricate trimming and pocket, is one such piece, showing the effect of embroidery worked in gold thread on ribbed silk (pl.57). The techniques on display here include satin stitch, spangles and undulating or spiralling heavy gold wire that has been flattened by a roller, known as *canetille*.

Plate 55
Charles Germain de Saint-Aubin
Design from *The Art of the Embroiderer*
Paris, 1770
Engraving, 34.9 x 23 cm
V&A: 68.C

Plate 56
Bord for a *veste*
French, *c*.1720–30
Pen and ink and brown wash,
20.4 x 42.6 cm
V&A: E.1944–1991

Plate 57
Veste shape
French, 1730–40
Embroidered silk
Galliera, Musée de la Mode, Paris

Bords

Life-sized embroidery schemes for items of clothing would be depicted on *bords*; the V&A possesses 16 finished *bords* for *vestes*, 23 for *gilets* and 6 for women's gowns, as well as unfinished, partly painted examples in graphite (pl.58). By 1780 the coat had developed skirts trimmed back to fit the figure and reveal the front of the waistcoat, and the embroidery tended to be concentrated where it could be seen, along the bottom front corner, including the pocket flap, or across the placket. Two larger *bords* from Lyon now in the V&A also have wide buttonholes for buttons mockingly described as being as huge as 'six-*livres* pieces' (pl.59).[10]

By the second half of the eighteenth century flower patterns were fanning outwards from the length of the centre-front openings of coats and waistcoats. These flower designs could either be naturalistic or fantastic, as on a *coupon* for a floral border made in Lyon around 1785 (pls 58, 59).

Fashion-conscious eighteenth-century dandies, known in France as *élégants*, often felt compelled to change their waistcoats several times a day and bought them by the dozen.[11] Doubtless made to meet this demand, the range of *bords* still in existence is extraordinary, their designs inspired by such diverse sources as nature, romance, antiquity, chinoiserie and even contemporary events.[12] The V&A has some particularly beautiful examples decorated with flowers, fighting cocks and deer (pl.60), and hounds hunting leopards (pl.61).[13]

Embroidery might also have a political message, as demonstrated by an example now in the National Museum of Ireland (pl.63).[14] Most extraordinary of all is a French *bord* of about 1789, with figures, possibly native Americans, guarded by French soldiers as they perform a dance with staves on a bridge; the water below is dotted with canoeists (pl.62). The scene may depict a 'carousel' or tournament at Versailles in 1662, when Louis XIV ordered Iroquois captives to sail their bark canoes on the palace lakes.[15] By the late eighteenth century opinions on legitimacy of enslaving non-Europeans had changed, so this *bord* is perhaps a contemporary political comment on a past era.[16]

Plate 58
Bord for a *veste* pocket
Lyon, 1785
Graphite and bodycolour, 17.8 x 33.9 cm
V&A: E.261–1937

Plate 59
Bord
Lyon, *c*.1785
Bodycolour, 24.7 x 14.6 cm
V&A: E.203–1930

Plate 60
Bord for a *gilet*
Lyon, *c*.1785
Bodycolour, 15 x 24.4 cm
V&A: E.253–1937

Plate 61
Gilet (detail)
French, 1790s–1800
Embroidered silk, 62.2 x 27.3 cm
V&A: 241–1899

Opposite
Plate 62
Bord for a *gilet*
Lyon, *c*.1789
Bodycolour, 14.8 x 25.6 cm
V&A: E.252–1937

Plate 63
Bord for a *gilet*
Lyon, *c*.1789
Bodycolour, 26.7 x 26.7 cm
© National Museum of Ireland,
Fitzhenry Gift

Women's dress

As fashion changed, so embroidery design had to adapt to new garment shapes and design trends. The origins of a new style of gown at the turn of the nineteenth century, in which light, usually white, straight dresses were worn over a natural figure, lay in the one-piece chemise dress, a late eighteenth-century garment of similar loose cut to the *levette* worn by Marie Antoinette in 1783.[17] This fashion spread to Britain, where white gowns, often of muslin, became fashionable from about 1795 to 1810.[18] The V&A Prints and Drawings collection contains a group of 48 English designs for women's dress in embroidered muslin dating from 1782–9.

Handwritten annotations on most of these designs appear to suggest that one individual was making a note of clients' names when taking an order. This design collection would have formed a retailer's archive, used in a bespoke fashion business. Often the garment for which a given design was destined is indicated in the inscriptions, or it may be evident from the arrangement of the pattern: right-angles were used for aprons and scalloped edges or festoons for the hems of gowns (pl.64).[19] A piece of English embroidery of the 1780s in a private collection with a similar festoon, embroidered in chain stitch, would have been intended for the petticoat to an open muslin gown or a skirt to a closed gown (pl.65).

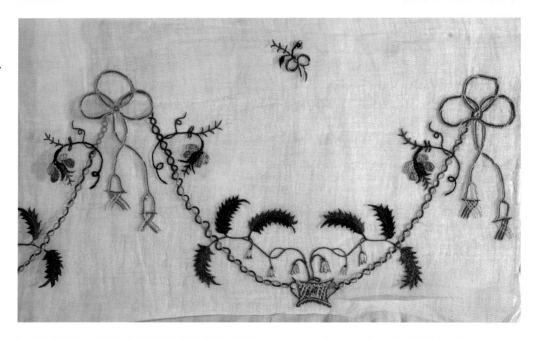

Plate 64
Design for embroidery
English, 1785
Pen and ink, 20.3 x 32.3 cm
V&A: E.224–1973

Plate 65
Petticoat to gown (detail)
English, 1780s
Embroidered muslin, 106 x 154.5 cm
V&A Loan: Moira Thunder

Plate 66
Morris & Co. Artworkers
Design for an embroidered yoke
c.1890s
Pencil, 18 x 30 cm
V&A: AAD/1990/6/file 1

Plate 81
Dress
English, *c.*1880
Embroidered silk
© Museum of London

Muslin

Muslin continued to be a popular fabric throughout the nineteenth century. Among other things it was used for the chemisette, a partially visible 'fill-in' worn under the low-cut bodice of a day dress, which by the 1860s had evolved into a long-sleeved blouse.

The designs of Mary Ann Hutton (see p.35) include a number of patterns for embroidery in whitework on chemisettes.

One design, inscribed 'high chemisette', has a high collar which would have stood up like a ruff;[20] the standard chemisette had a lower collar (pls 67–68). Hutton's designs included both lace and embroidered fashion items and accessories.

By the second half of the nineteenth century a move away from naturalistic representation in English embroidery had taken place, advocated by designers such as Letitia Higgin (1837–1913). In her *Art as Applied to Dress* (1885) Higgin wrote that 'embroidered or other trimming on dress must always be purely conventional in type; no representation of natural objects in relief'.[21] This type of stylized embroidery design, albeit with floral and foliate elements, is exemplified by the designs of William Morris and others of this period.

Plate 67
Chemisette (detail)
English, 1830–69
Embroidered lawn, 80 x 38.7 cm
V&A: T.210–1917

Opposite
Plate 68
Dresses from *La Belle Assemblée*
London, 1830
Handcoloured print, 21.3 x 14.3 cm
V&A: E.2325–1888

DINNER DRESS. CARRIAGE DRESS. PROMENADE DRESS.

Published by G.B. Whittaker, for La Belle Assemblee. No 65 New Series. May 1 1830.

Handkerchiefs

Handkerchiefs embroidered in coloured cottons began to appear from the 1850s onwards. In the 1860s it was usual to have 'morning handkerchiefs' in daily use, with colourful borders or corners to match a dress or its trimmings.[22] The right-angled arrangement of the flowers in a design by Mary Ann Hutton may be for an embroidered handkerchief (pl.69).

Plate 69
Mary Ann Hutton
Design for a handkerchief
*c.*1839 to late 1840s
Pen and ink and watercolour,
41.8 x 25.2 cm
V&A: D.1287–1901

Russian designs

Stylized floral decoration continued to be popular in embroidery at the beginning of the twentieth century. In Parisian fashion this was strongly influenced by traditional Russian embroidery design, in which regional dress was embroidered with motifs specific to its locality. There were several reasons for the Russian impact on Paris fashion. First, the renowned Ballets Russes dazzled Parisian audiences when they performed in native dress in 1909. In 1912 the couturier Paul Poiret (1879–1944) travelled to Russia and brought back with him embroidered tablecloths that subsequently inspired his fashion designs. In 1921 Gabrielle (Coco) Chanel (1883–1971) created an embroidery workshop in her villa at Garches, which became a centre for Russian émigrés; having learned embroidery in their childhood, many Russian refugees arriving in Paris found work in major couture houses such as Chanel.[23] In the aftermath of the Second World War, Russian embroidery became a substitute for other more expensive patterned fabrics.

Among the twentieth-century embroidery designs in the V&A is a group ranging in date from about 1900 to the 1970s by an unnamed Russian designer/embroiderer who worked in St Petersburg, Paris, and London (pl.70). Such designs are reflected in a chiffon day dress of about 1925 decorated with hand-embroidered bunches of flowers (pl.71).

Plate 70
Design for embroidery
Russian, *c*.1900–1925
Pencil, 35.2 x 24.6 cm
V&A: E.907.63–1994

Plate 71
Day dress
Paris, *c*.1925
Embroidered chiffon
V&A: T.65–1995

The Needlework Development Scheme

The Needlework Development Scheme (NDS), organized by four Scottish art schools – Aberdeen, Dundee, Edinburgh and Glasgow – was launched in 1934 with the aim of encouraging embroidery and improving the standard of design in Britain.[24] The NDS was funded by the thread manufacturers J. & P. Coats, and by the time it was disbanded in 1961 it had amassed over 3,000 textiles. Closed at the outbreak of the Second World War, the NDS resumed in 1944. At that point it was decided by embroidery experts that pieces of embroidery from overseas in the NDS

collection were superior to their British counterparts, so in 1947 Mary Kessell (1914–77), a leading British designer and war artist, was commissioned to create experimental designs to be reinterpreted in embroidery. Kessel's designs were considered so advanced that few art school embroidery artists could reproduce them; however, using various hand-embroidery techniques Marion Campbell from Bromley College of Art succeeded (pls 72, 73).[25]

When the NDS was closed in 1961, it was recognized that it had achieved its aims. Its collections were subsequently

distributed among organizations, universities and museums, including the Embroiderers' Guild, the V&A and the National Museums of Scotland.[26]

The revival of interest in embroidery in post-war Britain was encouraged by the publication of free transfer designs in popular magazines such as *Needlewoman and Needlecraft* (pl. 74). These designs could be simply ironed onto the textile for stitching, thus avoiding the complications of copying and scaling.

Plate 72
Mary Kessell
Design for yoke
1949
Coloured pencils on paper,
3.3 x 12.9 cm
V&A: Circ.334–1962

Plate 73
Marion Campbell
Child's dress (detail)
1949
Embroidered cotton,
43.2 cm
V&A: Circ.334B–1962

Plate 74
Needlewoman and Needlecraft,
no.102, cover
April 1965
29.3 x 22.2 cm
V&A: AAD/EPH/5/112

Needlewoman

No. 102 Two Shillings

Needlecraft

Among the embroidered items there is a very pretty shadow work cloth, a portion of which is shown on the left.

Modern and traditional pictures are the main theme in this issue. There are also many other ideas including knitting and crochet.

Bill Gibb

One later twentieth-century fashion designer for whom embroidered decoration was key to his work was Bill Gibb (1943–88). He showed a boyhood love of drawing at Fraserburgh Academy in Scotland, and in 1966 graduated top of his year at St Martin's School of Art. Having formed Bill Gibb Ltd with his partner Kate Franklin in 1972 and opened his first shop in Bond Street three years later, he became known for the vibrant colours and textile combinations of his designs.[27] In the words of one commentator,

> One of his greatest achievements was to blend fabrics and colour in a flamboyant and dramatic way, mixing pattern on pattern, check on floral, texture on texture, revolutionising the way designers treated cloth. His evening wear was an extravagant theatrical profusion of luxurious and sensuous fabrics, a fantasy of sparkle and shimmer.[28]

Embroidery was an integral part of Gibb's fashionable dress, with seams hidden beneath piping, beading, and braiding. Beadwork and embroidery were provided by Spangles, a couture beading company in London run by Lesley Coidan.[29] Gibb's final collection, in November 1985, combined silks, metallic thread, organza and net with sequins and machine embroidery (pl.75).

Plate 75
Bill Gibb
Evening Couture
1986
Black felt-tipped pen, colour wash and fabric samples on paper, 28.4 x 21 cm
V&A: E.522–1993
Bequeathed by the artist's friend, Philip Batty

Workers for Freedom

Embroidery designs feature in the work of Graham Fraser (b.1948) and Richard Nott (b.1947), founders of the cult label Workers for Freedom (WFF) in 1985.[30] They became known for its innovative fabrics and use of embroidery on clothes for both men and women (pl.76). Its hallmark garment is a shirt with black appliqué embroidered on white – or the reverse (pl.77) – which bears a striking resemblance to the Russian folk motifs popular in western Europe earlier in the twentieth century.[31]

Plate 76
Workers for Freedom
Ensemble
1990
Suit: cotton with machine embroidery
V&A: T.458–1995
Bequeathed by Simon Waldew
Waistcoat: appliqué embroidered linen
V&A: T.45–1992
Given by the designer

Plate 77
Workers for Freedom
Fashion design
1991
Pencil and watercolour on paper, 29.8 x 21.2 cm
V&A: E.2134–1992

ACCESSORIES

ACCESSORIES

Horsemanship and hunting

In centuries when horses were essential for transport, decorated horse trappings and saddlecloths offered an opportunity for embroidery. The V&A collection includes designs for ceremonial horse trappings by Paul Androuet du Cerceau (c.1630–1710), who published five suites of printed designs for embroidery from 1660–1710;[1] Daniel Marot, who produced a series of six printed designs for horse trappings;[2] and Margaretha Helm, who created designs for embroidered saddlecloths.

Paul Androuet du Cerceau's pen and ink and watercolour design of 1660–1710 (pl.81) is for one side of a horse trapping. The curve at the top of the design, if attached to its mirror image, would produce a semicircle to accommodate the horse's neck, while the straight edge on the right-hand side when joined to its counterpart would complete the symmetry of the pattern around the horse's chest.[3]

A printed design of about 1725 by Margaretha Helm shows the corner of a saddlecloth (pl.82) with foliate motifs; these are similar to the richly embroidered saddlecloth of an equestrian portrait of Louis XIV by René-Antoine Houasse (c.1645–1710) of c.1679 – where the horse's trappings are as richly embroidered as the French king's coat (pl.78). Helm matched her saddlecloth with printed designs for a pistol holder and an ammunition pouch (pl.80); these were republished in 1742 in *The Delights of the Art and Industry of the practising Needle*.[4]

Embroiderer Ludwig Koch was active in Bavaria or Saxony around 1755. In the V&A collection is an embroidered silk hunting pouch labelled in German: 'made by the master embroiderer LvdKoch [sic]'.[5] The outside of the pouch is embroidered in gold thread, while the inner pouches are embroidered with hunting scenes in coloured silks (pl.79).

Plate 78
René-Antoine Houasse
Louis XIV
c.1679
Oil on canvas, 93 x 75 cm
Musée des Beaux-Arts de Dijon

Plate 79
Ludwich Koch
Hunting pouch
Perhaps Bavaria or Saxony, c.1755
Embroidered silk, 53.3 x 48.2 cm
V&A: 306–1880

Ein Pistol hulster u. Patron Tasche.

Plate 80
Margaretha Helm
Design for a pistol holder and ammunition pouch
Nuremberg, *c.*1725
Engraving, 37 x 30 cm
V&A: E.3412–1932

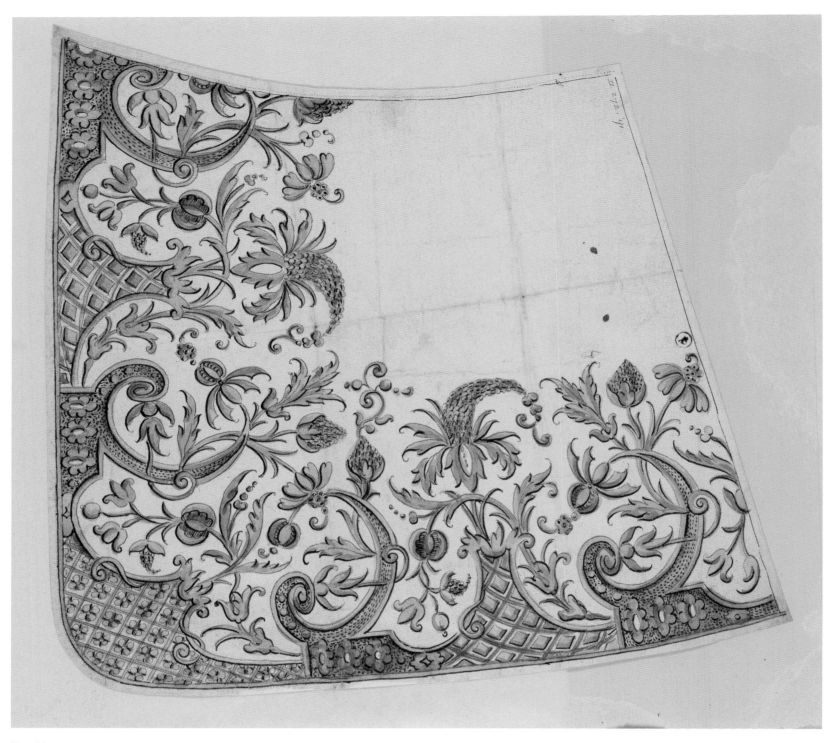

Plate 81
Paul Androuet du Cerceau
Design for a horse trapping
1660–1710
Pen and ink and watercolour on paper, 29.9 x 28.4 cm
V&A: D.272–1891

Plate 82
Margaretha Helm
Design for a saddlecloth
Nuremberg, *c*.1725
Engraving, 37 x 30 cm
V&A: E.3411–1932

Bibs

There could hardly be anything more different from the masculine world of hunting pouches than decorative bibs for babies, which were pinned to their linen swaddling strips, yet Margaretha Helm published designs for both. These included four printed designs for embroidered bibs (pl.83).[6]

The V&A also has a baby's linen bib made in England about 25 years earlier, decorated with double rows of couched braid sewn in a pattern of loops. This has four pinholes in the centre front, where the bib was attached to swaddling beneath (pl.84).

Plate 83
Margaretha Helm
Design for an embroidered bib
Nuremberg, *c.*1725
Engraving, 18.9 x 30.5 cm
V&A: E.5063–1905

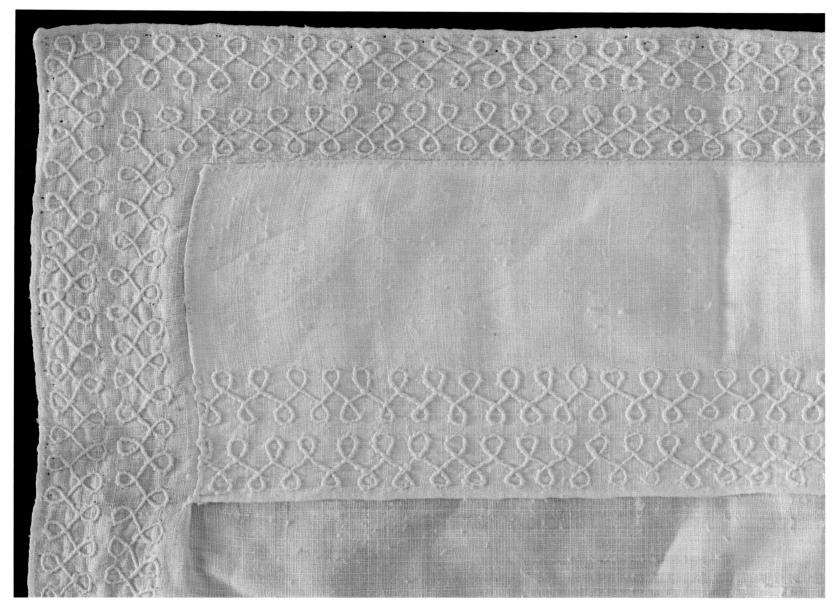

Plate 84
Bib (detail)
English, *c*.1700
Embroidered linen, 54.4 x 26.6 cm
V&A: Misc.323(6)–1984

Purses and bags

Embroidery was widely used to decorate purses in the seventeenth and eighteenth centuries. A popular design was the three-lobed purse with central clasp, exemplified by a dark blue satin version in the V&A, made in England in about 1680 and embroidered with raised flowers in gold and silk thread (pl.85). This shape remained popular for many decades: it reappears, for example, in Margaretha Helm's *Further Delights of the Art and Industry of the practising Needle* (1742).[7]

Helm's technical instructions for these 'women's bags' include 'sew with cross or satin stitch padded'. The designs were printed on a grid to facilitate the cross stitch recommended by the designer (pl.86).

In the V&A collection is a French hand-coloured engraved design by Antoine Chazal (1793–1854), one of 100 recorded for embroidered purses and other household items, drawn, engraved and published in Paris around 1825. This particular design, intended for beadwork embroidery, is for a purse based on a game bag or *gibecière* (pl.87).

The PDP collection contains a further 47 sheets of hand-coloured printed designs for embroidered purses made by various French designers in the 1820s.[8] The dressmaker Mary Ann Hutton annotated a design in her collection 'Muslin Bag 1841'; this was probably for whitework on muslin (pl.89). An example of this type of white bag is one decorated with appliquéd cambric on net (pl.88). A design made about ten years later, also by Hutton, shows a satin purse, flattened out and annotated with instructions, to be embroidered in couched braid (pl.90). Known as vermicular, this type of couched braid also appears on other fashion items of this date such as jackets and bags (pl.91).

Plate 85
Purse
English, *c*.1680
Embroidered silk, 39.5 x 8.9 cm
V&A: T.91–1935

Plate 86
Margaretha Helm
Designs for bags from *Further Delights…*
Nuremberg, *c.*1742
Engraving on paper. 18.9 x 28.5 cm
V&A: E.1153–1933

Plate 87
Antoine Chazal
Design for a game bag
French, *c.*1825
Hand-coloured engraving, 21.4 x 26.5 cm
V&A: E.4332–1910

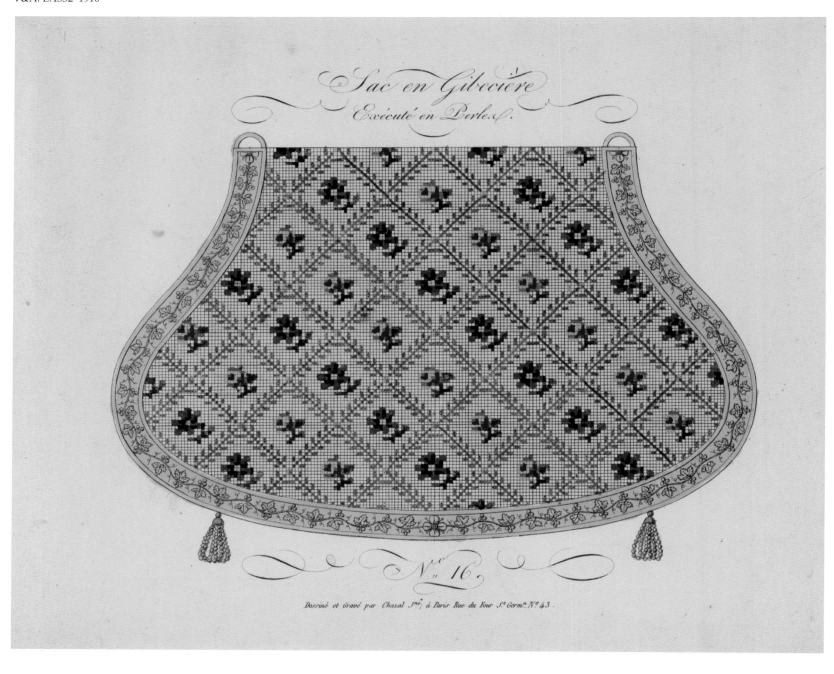

Left
Plate 88
Whitework bag
English, 1824
Appliquéd cambric on net, 20.5 x 21 cm
V&A: T.37C–1930
Given by Miss M. Ogilvy-Millar

Above
Plate 89
Mary Ann Hutton
Design for a muslin bag
1841
Pen and ink, 16.9 x 17.7 cm
V&A: D.1087–1901

Left
Plate 90
Mary Ann Hutton
Design for a purse
*c.*1850s
Pen and ink, 38.4 x 19.1 cm
V&A: D.1355–1901

Above
Plate 91
Bag
British, 1850–1900
Embroidered silk, 15.8 x 14.6 cm
V&A: T.1474–1913
Messrs Harrods Gift

Stockings and shoes

For many years it was the fashion for both men and women to wear stockings decorated with clocks. The clock was an embroidered, knitted or woven design, in contrasting or matching silk, in a vertical line just above the ankle; it would appear on the inner, outer, or even both sides of stockinged legs.[9] Embroidered gore clocks, with an additional tapering or triangular piece of fabric, were introduced around the 1670s to improve the fit of stockings produced on a knitting frame.[10]

The V&A has a number of designs for embroidered clocks, some of them with as many as 14 designs on a single sheet. Probably made in the eighteenth century, these were drawn on squared paper, perhaps printed in Nuremberg (pl.92).[11] A pair of early nineteenth-century British knitted silk stockings with embroidered clocks decorated with similar finials are also in the V&A collection (pl.95).[12]

Among the printed embroidery designs for shoes and slippers in the V&A collection are four for women's footwear, two for slippers and one, by Margaretha Helm, for slippers and a shoe.[13] The fourth of these (pl.93), published about 1725, shows the vamp (the front section of the shoe upper covering the toes and part of the instep) and one latchet (strap that fastens across the instep with a shoe-tie or buckle). Made in England at the same period, an embroidered vamp and quarter (back) in coloured threads on silk (pl.94) show what Helm's shoe designs might have looked like once embroidered, with the outlines of the pieces marked round the embroidery with graphite. The embroidered flowers, leaves and tendrils fill every part of the field, so that when made up, no part of the finished shoe would be left plain – as illustrated by an embroidered shoe of 1730–40 (pl.96).

Nearly a century later, Mary Ann Hutton produced slipper designs to be embroidered with braid and beads on velvet or cloth.[14] Similar designs were available to be copied from *The Lady's Newspaper* of 1847–56.

Other printed designs for slippers in the V&A collection include one by Louis Glüer (*fl.*1820–70), pattern painter, to be embroidered in Berlin woolwork. Printed in Berlin around 1840–50, the pattern was purchased in England and became part of an album of Berlin woolwork designs and sampler panels, probably compiled by an amateur embroiderer (pl.97). A pair of embroidered slipper fronts shows how such a design looks before the slippers are made up (pl.98). These were made just after the introduction of aniline (chemical) dyes, which increased the range of colours available to the embroiderer. Here the fashionably bright green and pink braid lines stand out crisply against the black felt fabric.

Plate 92
Designs for clocks
Possibly Nuremberg,
1750s–80s
Pen and ink, 37.2 x 45cm
V&A: 25690.10

Ein Schüh.

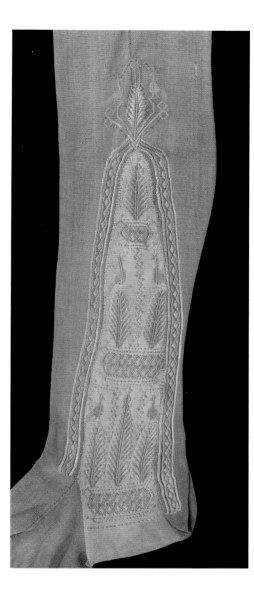

Opposite above
Plate 93
Margaretha Helm
Design for shoe, vamp and latchet
from *The Delights…*
Nuremberg, *c.*1725
Engraving, 19.2 x 28.9 cm
V&A: E.3403–1932

Opposite below
Plate 94
Shoe, vamp and quarter
English, early 18th century
Embroidered silk, 50.8 x 20.4 cm
V&A: 231–1908
Given by Miss C.E. Keddle

Left
Plate 95
Stocking with clock
British, 1800–30
Embroidered silk, 68.5 x 25.4 cm
V&A: 666–1898

Below
Plate 96
Shoe
English, 1730–40
Embroidered silk, 10.2 x 22.9 cm
V&A: Circ.995 & A–1924

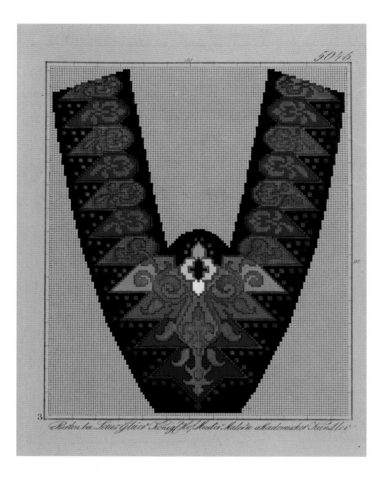

Plate 97
Louis Glüer
Design for a slipper
Berlin, 1840–50
Bodycolour on engraving, 23.4 x 19.3 cm
V&A. T.749.52–1974
Given by Miss Enys

Plate 98
Slipper fronts
English, c.1860
Embroidered felt, 38.7 x 58.5 cm
V&A: T.133 & A–1969
Given by Mrs E. Haynes

Braces

Men's fashion in Britain in the nineteenth century was generally much more sober than it had been in the eighteenth. However, during the 1840s and 1850s colourful embroidery continued to be popular where it could be worn discreetly, such as on braces and waistcoats.

Mary Ann Hutton's collection includes a design for men's braces inscribed in French 'to embroider on silk and canvas',[15] probably traced from an imported design (pl.99).

Also from this period is a pair of braces embroidered in Ireland in 1847, with a very similar fuchsia pattern (pl.100).

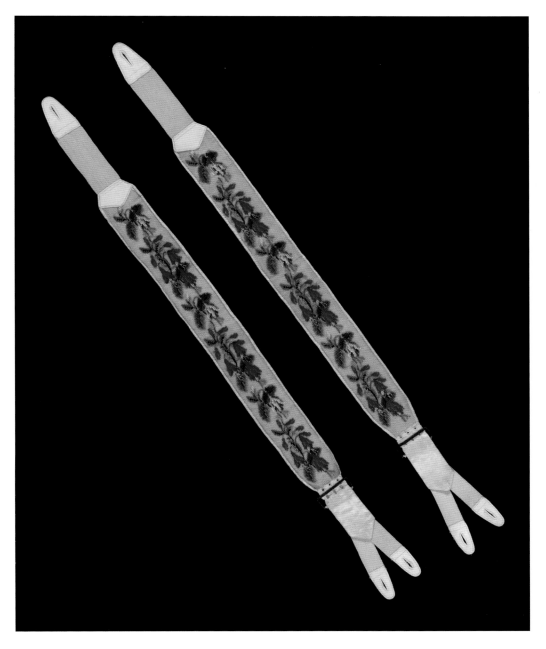

Plate 99
Mary Ann Hutton
Design for braces
French, 1850s
Pen and ink, 26 x 3.4 cm
V&A: D.1184–1901

Plate 100
Braces
Irish, 1847
Embroidered silk satin, 83.8 x 6 cm
V&A: T.213–1915
Given by Major and Mrs Mackay MacKenzie

Collars

Embroidered accessories for women in the nineteenth century included collars, which remained generally small and round from the 1840s until the 1860s. Raised satin stitch on white muslin was especially fashionable, for which collar patterns appeared in magazines such as *The Lady's Newspaper*.[16]

A series of designs from 1864 and 1865 in Hutton's collection show half-collars, from front to centre back (pl.101). These may be compared with a mid-nineteenth-century English collar embroidered in cotton whitework on net ground (pl.103).

Just a few years later, in 1875, Arthur Lasenby Liberty (1843–1917) founded his fashionable department store in London's Regent Street. The store soon became one of the most prestigious in London, and was a major influence on contemporary artists and designers. Among the designers whose work was showcased by Liberty's was Jessie Newbery (1864–1948), Head of Embroidery at Glasgow School of Art, who influenced an embroidery design for a child's dress collar published by Liberty's around 1905–9 (pl.102). The distinctive design of the stylized roses punctuating the edge and tips of the collar is characteristic of the new Art Nouveau style – which was so closely linked to Liberty's that it became known in some circles as the 'Stile Liberty'.[17]

Plate 101
Mary Ann Hutton
Designs for collars
1865
Pen and ink, each 20.2 x 4 cm
V&A. D.1025–1901

Plate 102
Liberty's
Design for a child's dress collar
*c.*1905–9
Lithograph, 28 x 34.5 cm
V&A: E.516–1975

Plate 103
Collar
English, 1830–70
Embroidered net, 22.1 x 4.7 cm
V&A: Circ.271–1925
Given by Brigadier-General J. Dallas

Caps

Until the end of the nineteenth century no outfit was complete without a cap or hat, worn by both men and women, at all times of day and night, across Britain and northern Europe. In private, informal dress, men wore nightcaps, often with a nightgown.

Nightcaps in the sixteenth, seventeenth and eighteenth centuries had a deep crown constructed from four conical sections stitched together, the border turned up to make a close-fitting brim.[18] These were often decorated with embroidery: a design of 1725 by Margaretha Helm shows two alternative designs for brims and crown (pl.109). She produced numerous other embroidery designs for nightcaps, whether with a deep, scalloped brim hiding the crown in a design[19] or more simply outlined, with decorative stems and flowers filling the pattern pieces. These were made available via publications such as *The Delights* and *Continuation of the Delights* (both published *c*.1725). Examples of caps in the V&A collections consist of two simple wing-shaped sides to be joined at a seam down the centre of the crown (pl.108).

Women wore embroidered caps both inside and outdoors over a 'settee' or 'double pinner', a close-fitting linen cap with lappets (long lace or linen streamers). These could be drawn up, as in an illustration from *Types of Clothing from the City of Augspurg* [*sic*], first published by Johann Merz of Augsburg in 1730 (pl.105).[20]

In 1688 Randle Holme (1627–99) described the linen cap: 'some draw the Settees so that the part which compasses the Head to the Ears shall stand up in Ruffs'. Two illustrations of women's heads in Holme's *Academy of Armory* show settees and linen caps worn beneath outer caps, the settees drawn tightly to resemble a ruff, following his description (pl.111).[21]

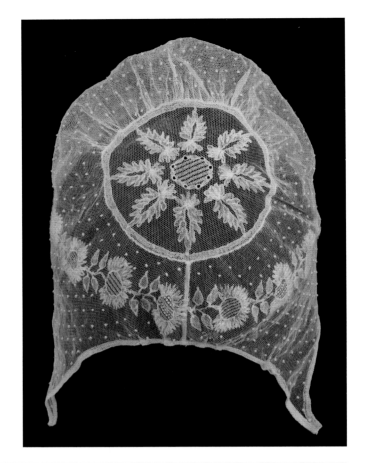

Plate 104
Cap crown
English, early 19th century
Embroidered net, 17.2 x 19.7 cm
V&A: Circ.137–1915

Plate 105
Johann Merz
Illustration from *Types of Clothing from the City of Augspurg* [*sic*]
Augsburg, 1730 (facsimile Berlin, 1924)
Phototype, 15.2 x 10.4 cm
V&A: L.897–1924

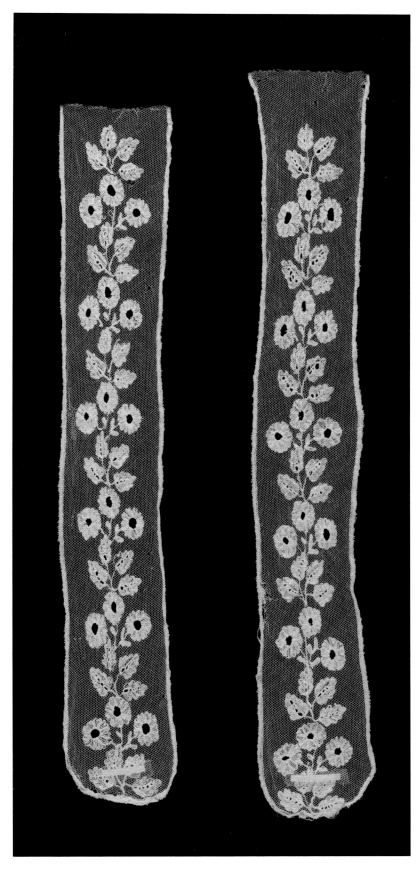

Plate 106
Mary Mansen (?)
Lappets
English, 1825–50
Embroidered net, 43.2 x 5.4 cm
V&A: E.205-205A–1968
Given by Mrs M. Cory

Plate 107
Fashionable Morning and Walking Dress
London, 1825.
Engraving, 18.2 x 11.2 cm
V&A: E.1479–1968

Fashionable Morning & Walking Dresses for June

The Morning Dress invented by Miss Pierpoint the Walking Dress by Madame de Montmore

Plate 108
Margaretha Helm
Designs for women's caps from *The Delights*…
Nuremberg, *c.*1725
Engraving, 42.8 x 30.5 cm
V&A: E.3395–1932

Frauen Inner Hauben.

Plate 109
Margaretha Helm
Designs for nightcaps from *Continuation of the Delights…*
Nuremberg, *c.*1725
Engraving, 29.8 x 39.9 cm
V&A: E.5067–1905

Caps were also worn by babies and children, and these were often delicately embroidered on fine fabric. One of many designs for whitework on muslin or net by Mary Ann Hutton fills a circular cap crown (pl.110), and is similar in shape to a child's cap embroidered with white cotton thread on machine-made net (pl.105).

Mary Mansen, a professional embroiderer active in England around 1827–65, built a collection of embroidery designs, of which 99 are in the V&A collection. The uniform style of many of her own designs suggests that she drew or copied from those in her collection; one of them, a design for a cap back (pl.112), is probably her original drawing. Most of Mansen's designs are for tambour work (embroidery on a tambour frame using a stitch similar to chain stitch) or whitework (any embroidery in white thread on a white fabric). These are complemented by accessories embroidered on machine-made bobbin net, possibly by Mansen herself: lappets, undersleeves and children's caps.[22] Among these is a pair of lappets of 1825–50, once joined, with a similar rose design to the cap back (pl.106). Joined lappets were sometimes worn as a headdress, as illustrated in a fashion plate of 1825 (pl.107).

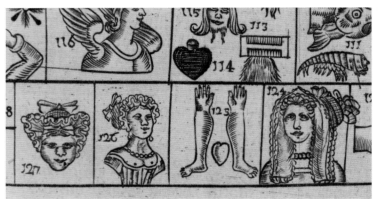

Plate 110
Mary Ann Hutton
Design for a cap crown
1840s–'50s
Pen and ink, 27.8 x 22.2 cm
V&A: D.931–1901

Plate 111
Randle Holme, *The Academy of Armory*
Chester, 1688
34 x 24 cm
V&A: 76.G.47

Plate 112
Mary Mansen
Design for a cap back
1827
Pen and ink, 17.3 x 14.1 cm
V&A: T.213.13–1968
Given by Mrs M. Cory

Embroidered caps were not restricted
to women and children: men, too, wore
ornately decorated caps, as witnessed by
a French embroidery design of about 1820
for a man's *calotte* or skull-cap (pl.113).
Consisting of four sections above a brim,
this was designed to cover just the top
of the head. The colour and shape look
forward to the early 1850s, when smoking
caps, to be worn with smoking jackets,
were a popular fashion for men (pl.114). A
very beautiful design by Mary Ann Hutton
shows the embroidered crown of a smoking
cap, with matching motifs for the side, to
be 'embroidered on Cloth & Silk with purse
silk in shades and gold thread' (pl.115).[23]

Plate 113
Maller the Elder
Design for a *calotte*
French, *c*.1820
Handcoloured engraving,18.6 x 22.9 cm
V&A: E.4350–1910

Gravé par Maller ainé, Editeur, Rue Michel-le-Comte, N.º 21.

Calotte.

N.º 6.   5.ème Année.

Plate 114
Smoking cap
British, c.1870
Embroidered felt, 9 x 17 cm
V&A: T.198–1968
Given by Mrs A.L.M. Fowler

Plate 115
Mary Ann Hutton
Design for a smoking cap crown
1850s
Pen and ink, 9.7 cm
V&A: D.1038–1901

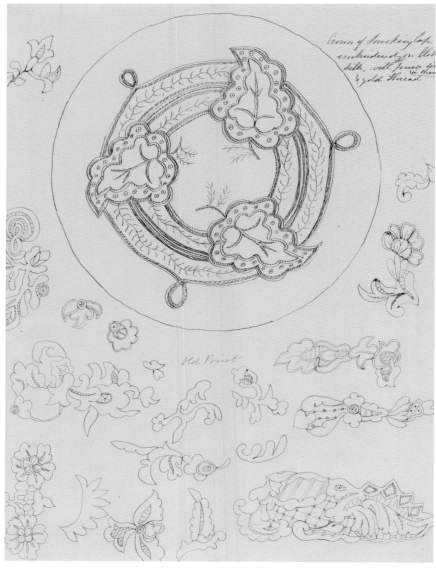

Kangol berets

Since the mid-twentieth century hats have gradually evolved from essential item of clothing to fashion accessory. Kangol berets are a case in point: founded in Cumbria, England, in 1938, the company was the major beret supplier to the armed forces during the Second World War. In 1964 it acquired the exclusive right to distribute headwear linked to the Beatles, and has managed to remain relevant to contemporary fashion.

Today the brand collaborates with 'talented, influential individuals' to achieve its objective: 'to satisfy a new generation of consumers', inviting artists such as Julie Verhoeven to produce a palette for the beret top. Verhoeven's design includes various media and techniques, including appliqué, studwork, imitation precious stones, printing – and embroidery (pls 116, 117).

Remarkably, when seeking a striking and unusual decorative effect, the producers of accessories today still turn to the ancient art of embroidery.

Plate 116
Julie Verhoeven
Design for a Kangol beret
2004
Mixed media on paper, 59.4 x 42.1 cm
V&A: E.545–2011
Given by the artist

Plate 117
Julie Verhoeven
Kangol beret
2004
Printing, appliquéd materials and machine-embroidery on cotton, 30 x 9.9 cm
V&A: T.128.1–2012
Given by Kangol Headwear Ltd

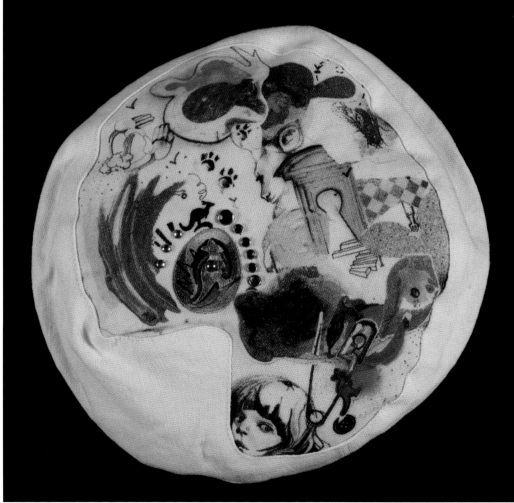

FURNISHINGS

FURNISHINGS

Love and privacy

Since the Middle Ages embroidery has been widely used for the decoration of furnishing fabrics. For example, bed-hangings, designed to keep out the cold and afford a degree of privacy in days when separate bedrooms were the preserve of the wealthy, offered an opportunity for lavish decoration.

The finest early beds had a wooden frame, often with posts at the corners, and, from the sixteenth century a flat top called a tester. This was usually surrounded by an inner and an outer valance, with the curtains running between them (pl.118). There were also valances on the two long sides of the bed, hanging from the frame to the floor; in France these were known as *pantes*, and in England as 'base valances'.[1] In the seventeenth century Matthias Mignerak designed patterns suitable for embroidery on canvas or net and appropriate for slips on a bed valance, such as that embroidered in England around 1650 to 1675, using coloured silks on linen canvas applied to silk satin (pl.37).

Other embroidery designs for bed furnishings in the V&A include two printed examples for embroidered valances by Georges Charmeton (1614–74), painter of architecture, engraved by Nicholas Robert (1614–85). These designs are from Charmeton and Robert's suite of six plates *All Sorts of Ornament such as … Pantes for Beds suitable for Embroidery* (*c*.1660)[2] and depict panels of grotesque ornament beneath which hang lambrequins, ornamental hangings designed in this case to cover the edge of the bed frame, alternating with tassels (pl.119). The effect could be highly lavish, as demonstrated by a Spanish valance of the first half of the seventeenth century embroidered with satin appliqué decoration worked in gold and silver thread (pl.120). The prolific French designer Paul Androuet du Cerceau (*c*.1630–1710) produced elaborate embroidery patterns, including two for borders composed of foliage and strapwork, possibly also for valances, one of which is illustrated here (pl.121).

Margaretha Helm's *Further Delights* (*c*.1742) reused patterns that were ultimately derived from sixteenth-century Italian examples. Although nearly two hundred years old, these designs were

still suitable for decorating bedlinen. The technical instructions in Helm's pattern book explained that the design could be embroidered in cross stitch or padded satin stitch. The printed designs are on paper printed with a grid that facilitated cross stitch (pl.122).[3] A design very similar to Helm's can be seen on a linen pillowcase of about 1700, perhaps made in Saxony or Bavaria (pl.123). This has a broad inserted band on one side embroidered in white linen thread, and a pattern comprised of a lattice filled with fleur-de-lys and foliated crosses.

In seventeenth- and eighteenth-century central Europe, 'letter pockets' were popular: these were textile hangings to which horizontal panels of embroidery were attached to form pockets for letters or other small items. A seventeenth-century example in the V&A has a loop for suspension and five pictorial panels (pl.124). The top rectangular panel

depicts winged figures on either side of an unidentified armorial shield, above which are the date and two sets of initials, probably of a husband and wife. The panel below shows the birth of Venus, and beneath that the standing figure of Venus, goddess of love, holding a flaming heart and an arrow; at her feet is her son, Cupid, flanked by putti shooting arrows. All symbolize love. The bottom panel shows the figure of Prudence holding a mirror and a snake,[4] while the top depicts Justice holding sword and scales. The embroidery was probably executed or commissioned by a bride on the occasion of her marriage in 1669.[5] A design for letter pockets by Margaretha Helm of about 1725 is also in the V&A collection (pl.125).[6]

Architect and designer Daniel Marot left France with his family in the wake of religious persecution after the Revocation of the Edict of Nantes in 1685. As Huguenot Protestants, the Marots were forced to leave

France and emigrated to the Netherlands. Daniel entered the service of Prince William of Orange and in 1688, when the Prince succeeded to the British throne, accompanied him to London. He worked for William and Mary at Hampton Court: the records of Mary's privy purse document annual fees paid to Daniel. Her payments to Daniel's brother Isaac Marot in 1694 are for textile designs, including 'designing and drawing 3 large pieces of silk during 3 weeks at 5s a day'.[7] It is possible that Isaac Marot may have been responsible for a surviving set of design drawings for a series of embroidered hangings.[8]

One record drawing and two design drawings attributed to Daniel Marot in the V&A have embroidered wall-hanging components associated with Queen Mary's Closet at Hampton Court Palace.[9] The set comprises eight embroidered hangings thought to be from this location, which divide into two groups of four. The first

Plate 118
Abigail Pett
Bed hangings
1680–1700
Crewel wool on linen and cotton, 197.5 x 102 cm
V&A: T.13B-C–1929
Given by Mr and Mrs W. J. H. Whittall

Plate 119
Nicholas Robert after Georges Charmeton
Designs for *pantes* for beds
c.1660
Engraving, 19.5 x 32.6 cm
V&A: E.1166–1937

Plate 120
Valance
Spanish, 1600–50
Embroidered velvet, 66 x 30.5 cm
V&A: 4894–1858

Plate 121
Paul Androuet du Cerceau
Design for a valance
*c.*1650s to 1710
Chalk, pen and ink and wash, 10.7 x 9.2 cm
V&A: D.273A–1891

Plate 122
Margaretha Helm
Designs from *Further Delights…*
Nuremberg, *c*.1742
Engraving, 18.5 x 28.4 cm
V&A: E.1136–1933

Plate 123
Pillowcase (detail)
Perhaps Saxony or Bavaria, 1700
Embroidered linen, 87.6 x 52.1 cm
V&A: 851–1901

group consists of three identical hangings, with a fourth lacking a bust at the top. The second group comprises three identical hangings and a fourth with the addition of a putto at the base.[10]

One of Daniel Marot's two drawings recording painted panels possibly designed by Alexis Loir (1640–1713), Parisian engraver and goldsmith, and imported for Montagu House (the Earl of Montagu's London mansion), features components of one of the embroidered hangings associated with Queen Mary.[11] The seated figures personifying Summer and Autumn, holding an overflowing cornucopia and a wheatsheaf and scythe respectively, were copied from the record drawing and reused for the embroidered hanging with the putto in the second group (pls 126 and 128). A design drawing for an embroidered or painted proposal, with a scale for the width and some initials for colours, includes components for the overall scheme of the second group of embroidered hangings.[12] This drawing and a second one are now thought to be by Daniel's brother, Isaac.[13]

The second of the two design drawings contains components for the first group of embroidered hangings (pls 127 and 130).[14] Elements from one record drawing by Daniel Marot and two design drawings perhaps by Isaac Marot therefore contributed to the first and second of these groups of hangings. It has been suggested that the drawings were the final solution to several proposals made for this room in Queen Mary's lifetime.[15] The embroidered hangings may have been incomplete until after her death, so were not hung by William III until the Closet was completed, around 1699–1700.[16]

Plate 124
Letter pockets
Perhaps Saxony or Bavaria, 1669
Embroidered silk, 66.1 x 27.9 cm
V&A: T.116–1956
Prendergast Bequest

Opposite
Plate 125
Margaretha Helm
Design for letter pockets from *Continuation of the Delights…*
Nuremberg, c.1725
Engraving, 19 x 29.9 cm
V&A: E.5083–1905

Brieff Caschen.

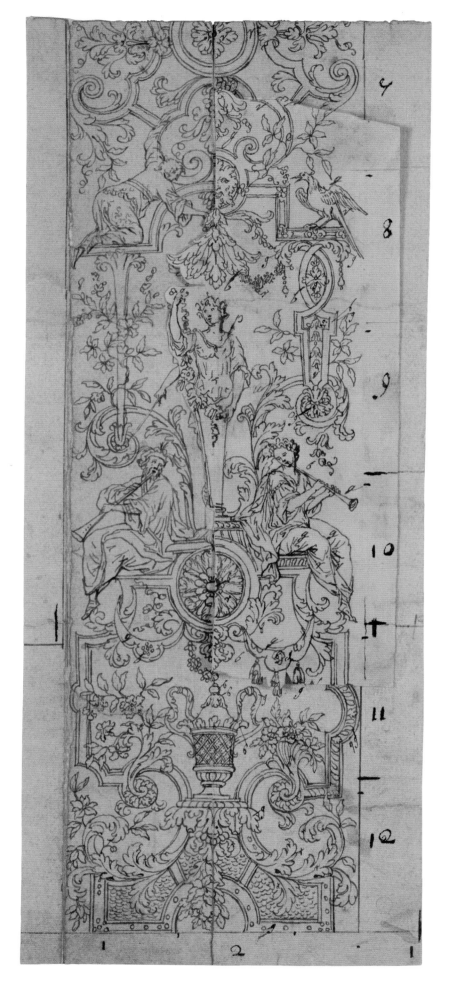

Berlin woolwork

Berlin woolwork designs were imported into England in small numbers until 1831, when Wilks, owner of a needlework shop at 186 Regent Street, London, began importing them in bulk from Berlin. Patterns were sold individually or as kits with coloured wools.[17] Many of the woolwork designs in the V&A bear the lettering 'Wilks', such as a brightly coloured design of a parrot probably intended for a fire-screen (pl.131). Another design in the collection, also embroidered in Berlin woolwork for a fire-screen panel, depicts an Australian sulphur-crested cockatoo, its plumage rendered in plush stitch (pl.134).[18]

By 1840 Berlin woolwork had become so popular that there were 14,000 different designs in circulation.[19] Wilks remained the main importer, although by 1854 Bath had eight Berlin wool warehouses, increasing to ten in 1866–7.[20] Exotic flowers were another favoured woolwork motif, often set against a dark background to enhance the richness of the colour palette. An arum lily and rose design for a chair (pl.133) typifies this style, while a woolwork chair cover in the same style but depicting full-blown roses has now faded but its light pink/brown colour would originally have been a darker red (pl.132).[21]

Plate 131
F.W. Lusch
Design for a fire-screen
Berlin, 1825–50
Handcoloured engraving, 36.5 x 35.7 cm
V&A: E.1488–1959

Plate 132
Chair
English, c.1845
Berlin woolwork, 96 x 48 cm
V&A: W.93–1921

Plate 133
Carl Wicht
Design for a chair back
Berlin, c.1850
Handcoloured engraving, 32.8 x 26.7 cm
V&A: E.517–1935
Given by Mrs W.F.A. Ellison

Opposite
Plate 134
Fire-screen panel
English, 1850s
Berlin woolwork, 91 x 81 cm
V&A: T.95–1970
Bequeathed by Brigadier W.E. Clark
CMG DSO through the Art Fund

William Morris

After Morris & Co. came under the sole ownership of William Morris in 1875, the company became a leading supplier of embroidery designs. Perhaps the most admired pattern of the 1870s and the early 1880s was the 'Artichoke', commissioned and embroidered by Ada Phoebe Godman (from 1877 to 1900) as wall hangings for her home, Smeaton Manor (pl.136). The design was used several times and its copyright did not, as with other commissions, remain the property of the original client.[22]

There is one original design by Morris in the PDP (pl.135) and a copy in the AAD that may be by John Henry Dearle (1860–1932), who also designed embroidery for Morris & Co. An inscription on the reverse of the copy reads 'Mrs Coronio 10 Holland Park'. This refers to Aglaia Coronio, née Ionides (1834–1906), a client and friend of Morris. A version of 'Artichoke' was embroidered by another Morris client, Margaret Beale (1847–1936), amateur embroiderer and neighbour of the Coronio and Ionides families in Holland Park, for her country home, Standen in East Sussex.[23]

Morris & Co. produced embroidery kits comprising ready-traced designs on either Manchester cloth (cotton) or silk, complete with specially dyed embroidery silks. They sold these in their showrooms in Oxford Street, London, and John Dalton Street, Manchester.[24] A ready-traced design of about 1890 for 'Olive and Rose' on glazed cotton has a corner painted in bodycolour as a guide to the embroiderer (pl.137). An unfinished embroidered cushion cover with this design is in the V&A's collection.[25] 'Olive and Rose' could also be used as a screen mounted in a cheval frame, allowing it to be swivelled. This embroidery is illustrated twice, once as a finished screen, in the firm's *Embroidery Work* catalogue as

late as 1913. The catalogue explained that 'darning work is supplied ready traced and started'.[26] These embroidery kits overtook Berlin woolwork in popularity.

May Morris learnt from her parents, both excellent embroiderers, and was trained at the South Kensington School of Design from 1880 to 1883. In 1885, aged just 22, she took over the running of the company's embroidery department.[27] In 1893 she published *Decorative Needlework*, a beginner's guide to embroidery, declaring that: 'Symmetry, order and balance are above all things essential, and ... no attempted copying of the painter's art ... in such dissimilar and insufficient materials is permissible.'[28] Her statement forbids copying famous paintings in Berlin woolwork.[29] Her daily work involved embroidering her father's patterns, ranging from wall hangings to embroidery kits, and also designing and embroidering her own work. Like her father, May Morris was part of the Arts and Crafts movement that emerged in the 1860s, and she contributed to their exhibitions between 1888 and 1931. Unlike her father's designs, May's used tonal contrast and, sometimes, perspective. Instead of stylized subjects such as scrolling acanthus, it was the flowers and birds of the garden and hedgerow that inspired her (pl.139).[30] She bequeathed eight embroidery designs to the V&A.[31]

May Morris's naturalistic approach to embroidery and her skilful execution of designs influenced a generation of embroiderers in the early 1900s, including Jessie Newbery (1864–1948) and the Glasgow School.[32] Phoebe Traquair designed a tea cosy depicting British fauna and flora to be embroidered in silk and wool (pl.138).

Plate 135
William Morris
'Artichoke', design for an embroidered wall hanging
1877
Watercolour, 104 x 37 cm
V&A: 65–1898
Given by Mrs Morris

Opposite
Plate 136
Ada Godman after William Morris
'Artichoke', embroidered hanging
1877
Silk on linen, 213 x 150 cm
V&A: T.166–1978

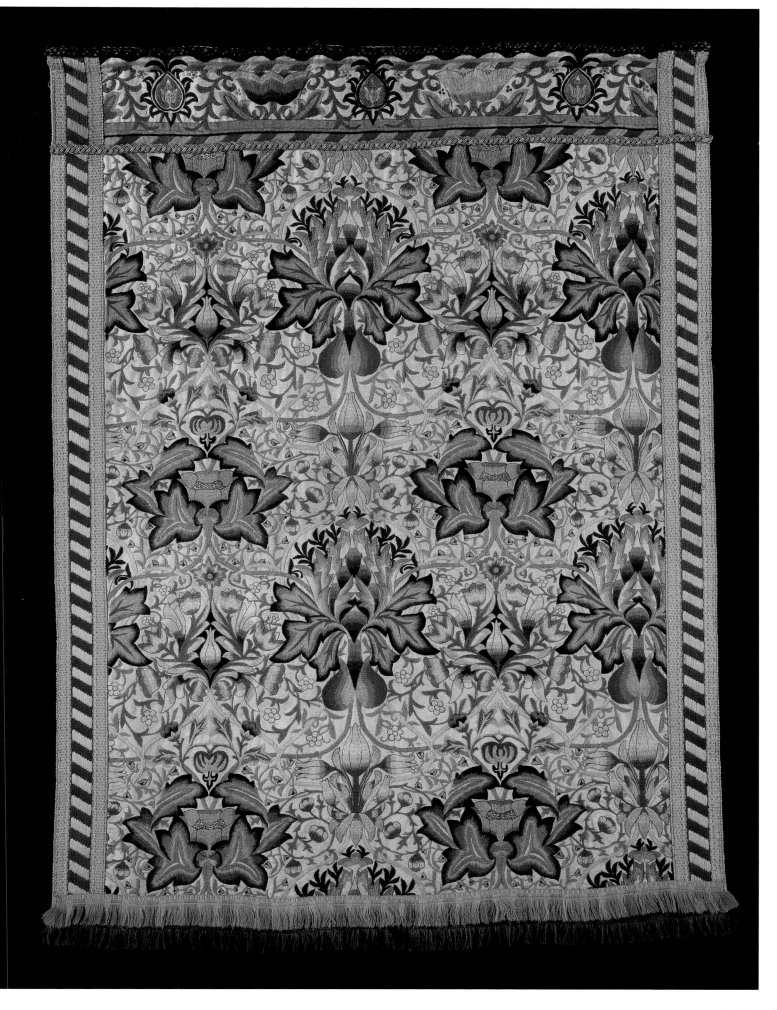

Plate 137
Morris & Co, Artworkers
'Olive and Rose' embroidery design
*c.*1890
Pen, ink and watercolour on cotton, 62.1 x 62.3 cm
V&A: AAD/1990/6/file 3

Plate 138
Phoebe Traquair
Design for a tea cosy
*c.*1890
Pencil, 26 x 41.1 cm
V&A: E.1017–1976

Plate 139
May Morris
Design for a chair-seat
*c.*1885–1931
Chalk and bodycolour, 67.9 x 95.3 cm
V&A: E.960–1954
Bequeathed by the artist

Edward Burne-Jones

One of the leading artists of the Pre-Raphaelite movement, Edward Burne-Jones, created a design for an embroidered panel depicting the personification of Love (pl.140). The inscription, 'Love which moves the sun and other stars', is taken from the last line of the *Divine Comedy* by Dante Alighieri (1265–1321).[33] Burne-Jones created the design in the 1880s for his close friend Lady Frances Horner (1854/5–1925), patron of the arts and amateur embroiderer. A panel that she embroidered after Burne-Jones's design is now preserved in the church of St Andrews, Mells, Somerset.[34]

Plate 140
Edward Burne-Jones
Love
1880s
Bodycolour, 210.8 x 107.2 cm
V&A: E.838–1937
Given by The Hon. Mrs Margaret Post

The Needlework Development Scheme

In the twentieth century the popularity of embroidery for furnishing diminished but it did not disappear altogether. In 1961 a design and sample for embroidered curtains (pl.141) were created under the Needlework Development Scheme (see p.64). The design, a sunflower in broad outline, is a block print on linen, accompanied by a sample showing how the motif could be embroidered in a variety of different stitches. The embroidery on the finished curtain, with the bottom of the border in open Cretan stitch, is enhanced by its grey Moygashel Irish linen ground (pl.142).

Plate 141
Needlework Development Scheme design and sample
1961
Print and embroidered print on fabric, 30.8 x 41.3 cm
V&A: Circ.297-A–1962

Plate 142
Needlework Development Scheme
Curtain
1961
Embroidery on Moygashel Irish linen, 156.2 x 71.1 cm
V&A: Circ.297–1962

Table decorations

Among early embroidery designs for table linen in the V&A collection is a right-angled design from the pattern book made by Lunardo Fero in 1559, probably for the corner of a tablecloth or another household textile (pl.143).[35] Two editions of Margaretha Helm's pattern book *The Delights of the Art and Industry of the practising Needle* (1725 and 1745) include a group of nine early eighteenth-century designs for tablecloths, entitled *Täffelein* or 'little tables', for formal entertainment. These realistic depictions of flowers or fruit were intended to be embroidered 'on canvas, taffeta, or silk in long and short stitch, satin stitch, padded satin stitch, and cross stitch in all kinds of dyed silks or thread'.[36]

Of much later date is the V&A's collection of early twentieth-century Russian designs for borders, tablecloths and covers (pl.144). Two printed embroidery designs for household linen were published as supplements to the August and November issues of the monthly periodical *Modes et Travaux* (Paris 1960), with patterns covering both sides of the sheet.[37] The designs in the August issue included patterns for a tablecloth decorated with sweet peas and a long bag with folding flap to contain a baguette, economically laid out so that the tablecloth overlapped the bag (pl.145).

A tablecloth design called 'Pekin' published in the April 1965 edition of *Needlewoman and Needlecraft* was available, 'traced on good quality cream linen', from most needlework shops (pls 146, 147). This commercial pattern displays little of the Needlework Development Scheme objective of challenging and raising the standard of embroidery design.

Plate 143
Lunardo Fero
Pattern book
Venice, 1559
Pen and ink and watercolour on paper, 19.4 x 15 cm
V&A: E.1940.12–1909

Plate 144
Tablecloth design
Russia, *c.*1900–10.
Watercolour, 50.5 x 64.7 cm
V&A: E.910.11–1994

Plate 145
Designs for household linen from *Modes et Travaux*
Paris, 1960
Lithographs, 71.5 x 111.8 cm
V&A: E.1351.2–1986

Plates 146, 147
'Pekin' tablecloth design from *Needlewoman and Needlecraft*, no. 102, April 1965
29.3 x 22.2 cm
V&A: AAD/EPH/5/112

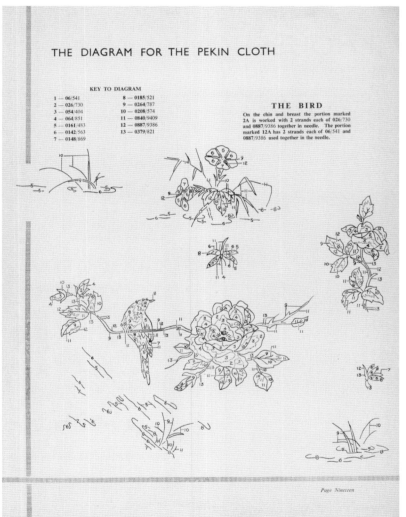

The sea

A popular source of inspiration for furnishing embroidery in the 1930s was the seaside. An embroidered panel by Vanessa Bell (1879–1961) of 1935 features shells before a seascape,[38] while Allan Walton's (1892–1948) designs of about 1938 for embroidered chair seats, 'Summer' and 'Autumn' (pls 148, 149), have a maritime theme. The panel by Bell and Walton's 'Summer' have similar dotted areas in the foreground and border respectively. Bell's panel was designed for the furnishings of Charleston, West Sussex, her country home from 1916, while Walton's seat designs are from a set of four representing the seasons. 'Summer' is a trompe-l'oeil view through a cave mouth to seashells, one of which looks ambiguously like an ice-cream cone (pl.148). The incongruity of sitting on an ice cream cone echoes the unexpected juxtapositions of 1930s Surrealism.[39] Lady Glyn (1881–1958) transformed Walton's designs into embroidered chair seats (pl.150), of which two are now in the V&A's collection; the remaining pair were given to the Women's Institute Headquarters, Denman College, Buckinghamshire.[40]

Associations with the sea permeate the embroidered 'Waves' counterpane (pls 151, 152), cushions and bolster designs by Paddy Killer (b.1949), who exhibits with the '62 Group, founded in 1962 to encourage experimental embroidery and the use of mixed media. The 'Waves' designs were part of a private commission in 1993 that included a bed with wave-shaped headboard by Cebuan de la Rochette. Free machine embroidery on the counterpane depicts the vermicelli pattern for which Killer is famous, and is complemented by drawing, painting and marbling on Antung Chinese silk.

Plate 148
Allan Walton
'Summer' chair seat design
*c.*1938
Pencil, watercolour and bodycolour on paper,
45.1 x 53.3 cm
V&A: E.5327–1960
Given by Freda, Countess of Listowel

Plate 149
Allan Walton
'Autumn' chair seat design
*c.*1938
Pencil, watercolour and bodycolour on paper,
41.6 x 53.3 cm
V&A: E.5328–1960
Given by Freda, Countess of Listowel

Plate 150
Lady Glyn after Allan Walton
'Summer' embroidered chair seat
*c.*1938
Wool on canvas, 41.2 x 52.1 cm
V&A: T.1A–1959
Given by Lord Glyn

Plate 151
Paddy Killer,
'Waves' counterpane design
1993
Pen and ink, gold felt-tipped pen,
watercolour and collage, 59.3 x 41.7 cm
V&A: E.82-2013

Plate 152
Paddy Killer
'Waves' counterpane
1993
Machine embroidery, drawing and painting
on silk, 250 x 250 cm
Paddy Killer

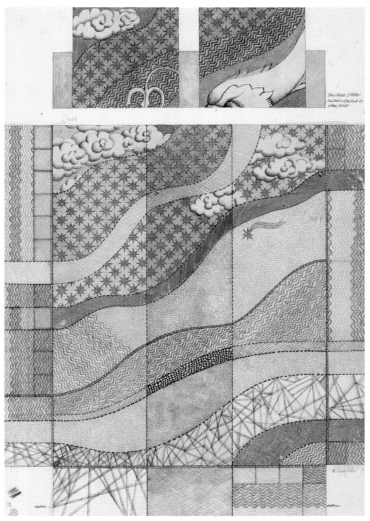

Notes

Introduction

1. D. Pilgrim, 'Director's Foreword', *Disegno: Italian Renaissance Designs for the Decorative Arts* (New York 1997), pp.vii–viii.

2. Gascoigne 1986, no.19.

3. Nevinson 1950, p.xvii; Lotz 1933, pp.35, 112 and 128.

4. Levey 1983, p.6.

5. Ibid., p.6. A facsimile of a French reprint of Vinciolo, entitled *Les singuliers et nouveaux pourtraicts … pour toutes sortes d'ouvrages de lingerie* (published in 1592) is in the V&A. It is not known where a copy of the English translation exists.

6. Johann Siebmacher, *Newes Modelbuch in Kupffer gemacht, darinnen allerhand Arth newes Model von Dün, Mittel, und dick aussgeschnidener Arbeit auch andern künstlichen Neh werck zu gebrauchen mit vleiss inn Druck verfertigt / New Pattern Book, printed with copperplate … in which all kinds of new patterns from … point, and thick cutwork and other artistic needlework to use with worsted are produced in print* (Nuremberg 1604).

7. Rosina Fürst, *Neues Model-Buch. Anderer Theil. Von unterschiedlicher Art, von schönen Nädereyen Ladengewürck und Paterleins-Arbeit New Pattern Book / Next part. Of different kinds, of beautiful Needlework, Drawloom work and Father linen work* [ecclesiastical linen] (Nuremberg 1666).

8. Levey 1983, p.18 and pl.96 for a *lacis* cover similar to Mignerak's border designs. Mignerak's pattern book does include plates lettered 'trimmings made with a bobbin' (Levey 1983, p.10, n.27). Six plates are lettered 'Passements faicts en Fuzeau'. Matthias Mignerak, *La Pratique de L'Aiguille industrieuse du très excellent Milour Mathias Mignerak, Anglois, ouurier fort expert en toutes sortes de lingeries où sont tracez diuers compartimens de carrez tous differans en grandeur et inuention, avec les plus exquises bordures, desseins d'ordonances qui sesoient veuz iusqu'à ce iourd'hui, tant poetiques, historiques, qu'autres ouurages de poinct de rebord… / The Practice of the industrious needle of the most excellent Milord Mathias Mignerak, Englishman, great expert in all sorts of domestic linen in which a variety of square compartments of differing size and type are represented by lines and points, with the most exquisite borders,* designs with compositions that have not been seen until today, more poetical and historical than other works of double running stitch … (Paris 1605)

9. Brooks 2004, p.40, no.7. V&A: T.134–1929.

10. The borders by Mignerak are V&A: E.2268–1931, E.2276–7–1931 (both borders) in plates from an original edition (94.G.9) in PDP. Shorleyker also copied Mignerak's seven plates lettered 'trimmings made with a bobbin'. These designs are from plates Siij; Siiij; T; Tij; Tiij and Tiiij in the facsimile of Mignerak in the NAL, V&A: RC.H.36.

11. Palliser 1902, p.20, n.16.

12. Levey 1998, p.A.2.

13. The other option is pricking to transfer the design to a support so that it could be used to make bobbin lace.

14. Paganino, 1878–80, originally published in 1527.

15. Rosina Fürst, *Model-Buchs Dritter Theil von unterschiedlichen Vögeln, Blumen, und Früchten, wie dieselbige zum Weiss-Nehen … oder andern dergleichen Arbeit, nach eines jeglichen Belieben anzuwenden / Pattern book third part: a variety of birds, flowers, and fruit, to sew in whitework … or any similar work, use each as you like* (probably Nuremberg 1676).

16. Hackney 2006, pp.23.

17. Lomas 2001, no.135, pp.151–2 and no.75, pp.83–4. Ramah Judah collected designs for her own purposes but not for employment.

18. Jean-Baptise Pillement, *L' Œuvre de Jean Pillement / The Work of Jean Pillement* (Paris 1767) Gordon-Smith 2006, p.173.

19. Jean-Baptiste Pillement, *Recueil de differentes Fleurs de Fantasie dans le gout chinois, Propres aux Manufacture d'etoffes de Soie et d'Indienne / Collection of various Fantastic Flowers in the Chinese taste suitable for the Manufacture of Silk textiles and painted and printed Cotton fabrics* (London 1760).

20. Pierre Vallet, *Le Jardin du Roy, Très Chrestien Loys, Roy de France et de Navare dedie a la Royne Mere de sa mt… / The Garden of the very Christian King Loys … King of France and Navarre dedicated to the Queen Mother …* (Paris 1624). See Saunders 1995, p.55.

21. Pierre Vallet's recipe for colour included 'Avignon grain when left to steep in a water and alum solution, all other colours are vivid enough [*sic*]'. He advises the reader to wash the paper (for painting on) with alum solution and without wiping, leave it to dry.

22. Design inscribed 'Mrs Hutton – Kate's Dress 1823' (V&A: D.1283–1901).

23. Kelly 1856, p.313; Harrison, Harrod & Co. 1862, p.547; Kelly 1866, pp.1039, 1229; Morris 1870, pp.403, 433; White 1878–9, pp.810, 1039; Kelly 1883, pp.470, 724; Kelly 1889, pp.583, 836; White 1890, p.976; Kelly 1893, p.636; Kelly 1897, pp.697, 942.

24. Patterns of insertion, muslin, embroidery, etc, published by Anbert, Martin, Helot etc., Paris: V&A: E.2036–2273–1901.

25. Keene 1826; Wooster 1866–7, Trades Directory and pp.445–8.

26. Wooster 1864–7, pp.31, 59, 70, 89, 111, 124, 140, 143, 206, 213, 222, 247.

27. Smith 1865–6; V&A: D.1029-31–1901.

28. *Morris & Co.* 1870, p.433; Tomlinson, 1983.

29. Ajmar-Wollheim and Dennis 2006, p.161; Levey 1983, p.6; Brooks 2004, p.7.

30. Thunder 2010; Margaretha Helm *Further Delights* (Nuremberg, *c*.1742).

31. See Parker 1984 for full discussion of embroidery subjugating women.

32. Brooks 2004, p.7; Morrall and Watt 2008, p.23.

33. Browne 2003, pp.7–9.

34. Ajmar-Wollheim and Dennis 2006, p.161.

35. For Fero: Ajmar-Wollheim and Dennis, p.365, no.202; Novello: V&A: D.1751.1–1908.

36. Identical patterns are: Fero E.1940.8–1909 and Novello D.1751.12–1908, except for the top motif. Pelican in her piety: Fero E.1940.7–1909 and Novello D.1751.9–1908. Surround to coat of arms: red acanthus and arabesques in Fero E.1940.27–1909, orange acanthus and arabesques in Novello D.1751.17–1908.

37. The families are von Wimpffen; von Kressensstein, and Schlüsselfelder and a fourth coat of arms is of Melchior Metschters, the late Nuremberg theatre official and his widow, Anna Marien. The latter are only listed in the dedication of another copy of this pattern book V&A: 95.O.13. Fürst, 1666 (see note 7 above).

38. Nevinson 1936, p.281. John Taylor, 'In Praise of the Needle', *The Needles Excellency: A New Booke wherein are divers admirable Workes wrought with the Needle. Newly invented and cut in Copper for the Pleasure and Profit of the Industries* (London 1636, pp.B, B2–3 verso). The poem mentions Katherine of Aragon, Queen Mary I, Queen Elizabeth I, Mary Queen of Scots, and the more contemporary aristocratic ladies, Lady Mary, Countess of Pembroke (1561–1621) and Lady Elizabeth Dormer, who married Robert Dormer in 1590. He died Lord Dormer in 1616. This pattern book includes designs mostly for cutwork.

39. 'J imite [*sic*] de Sy pres la nature / En nuant ces mignardes fleurs / Qu'outre le traict de pourtraicture / L'on en admire les couleurs'('I imitate nature so closely in depicting these delicate flowers as well as their delineation one admires the colours').

40. The designs in the V&A complement those in other collections, including the Musée Historique des Tissus in Lyon; Musée des Arts Décoratifs in Paris; the British Museum, London, Waddesdon Manor, Buckinghamshire; the National Museum of Ireland, Dublin; the Metropolitan Museum of Art, New York, and the Cooper-Hewitt, National Design Museum, New York.

41. Baudis 2008 (the dating of related designs in this book are based on Baudis's dating system.)

42. The trade card depicts the master embroiderer showing a male client an embroidered waistcoat while his female companion looks at designs. The trade card is at Waddesdon Manor. Baudis 2008, p.179, pl.3.37.

43. Lemire, 1997, pp.50, 56, 67 quoted in Thunder 2006, p.88.

44. Harvey 1991, p.22.

45. Crawford 2004, accessed 7 June 2013.

46. Cumming 2004, accessed 7 June 2013.

47. Rothstein 1990, pls 190–1, 238, V&A: T.391–1971, p.9; 5985.13.

48. Scheuer 1983, pp.38, 67, 68. See *dessin marqué* in Saint-Aubin 1770, p.35.

49. V&A: E.218A–1930, E.216–1930, E.219–1930, E.211–1930, E.3942–1911.

50. Measurements: 9.5 × w.9.9 cm, V&A: D.1218–1901.

51. 1881 England Census, Torquay.

52. Morrall and Watt 2008, figs 4–10, p.71; figs 5-10, p.93; cat.6, p.123; cat.25, p.159; cat.46, p.201; cat.58, p.227; cat.62, p.235; cat.65, p.241; cat.66, p.243; cat.69, p.248; cat.70, p.251; cat.73, p.263; cat.76, p.269; cat.77, p.273; cat.79, p.277; cat.80, p.279; cat.84, p.287; cat.85, p.289. Saunders 1995, pp.32–6.

53. Saunders 1995, p.29.

54. The second half of *Schole-house for the Needle* has a title page stating the range of content and suggestions for embroidery: 'Here followeth certaine patternes …sundry sorts of spots, as flowers, birds and fishes & c. and will fitly serve to be wrought, some with gould, some with silke, and some with crewel, or otherwise at your pleasure.'

55. Levey 1998; Barker 1988.

56. Arber 1877, p.145. Shorleyker published an earlier edition of 1624, a copy of which survives in the Musée des Arts Décoratifs in Brussels. See Barker 2000, p.57.

57. Morrall and Watt 2008, pp.168–9; Nevinson 1968 p.3; Barker 1988, p.50. Barker 2000, pp.13, 119.

58. L.E. Miller 1998, pp.272–81.

59. Botanical studies have been in collection of the Musée des Tissus since before 1891 when it was called the Musée d'Art et d'Industrie Rhône (1858–64). Such studies were among over 1,350 preparatory sketches for designs and embroideries that were acquired from the Bergeret and Bellemont purchase in 1864.

60. V&A: 25927 (EO.92). Privat-Savigny (2010), p.10

61. Levey 1989, p.6.

62. Berlin manufactories: Hertz & Wegener; Louis Glüer Konig; Knechtel & Co.; Heinrich Kuehn; A. Nicolai; A. Todt; Carl F.W.Wicht; L.W. Wittich. Paris manufactories and magazine: N. Alexandre & Cie Maurice Lajeunesse; *Maison des Desmoiselles* (1856–7); Vallardi. British magazines: *The Englishwoman's Domestic Magazine* (1869); *The Young Ladies Journal*. Strasbourg manufactory: Silbermann.

63. Cumming 2004; Hulse 2010, pp.20–1, 74, no.14.

64. V&A: T.207–1970.

Fashion

1. Domenico da Sera, *Opera nova composta per Domenico da Sera … dove si insegna a tutte le nobili & leggiadre giovanette di lavorare di ogni sorte di punti: curire: recamare, & far tutte qlle belle opere … / New work compiled by Domenico da Sera … to all the noble and elegant young women wherein such decoration to work with all sorts of stitches: sewing: embroidery, & all such beautiful work…* (Venice 1543).

2. Amalia Beer, *Wol-anständige … Frauen Zimmer-Ergötzung, in sich enthaltend Ein … Neh-und Stick-Buch … von Frau Amalia Beerin Respectable … / Delightful Women, in which is contained a … Sewing and Embroidery Book …* (Nuremberg *c*.1715–23).

3. 'Mehr einer züm Sticken Bilder Stich'. This engraving exists in two forms in the collection of the Word & Image Department, this one is loose with the lettering and the other has its lettering erased in a bound compilation of assorted prints masquerading as an Italian pattern book published in 1694 with the title *New Patterns of Embroidery / Nuovissimi Esemplare di Ricami*. It is possible to pinpoint the date of publication of the pattern book *Respectable … Delightful Women in which is contained a … Sewing and Embroidery Book … to between 1715 when Amalia married Johann Gabriel Beeren and her death in 1723. Doppelmayr 1730, p.275. The title page (loose) is catalogued in the Prints Micromedia online catalogue under Beer's maiden name 'Pachelblin', V&A: 24365A.

4. Thornton 1965, p.158.

5. Buck 1984, p.188.

6. Delpierre 1983, p.184. Baudis 2008, p.iv. The glossary terms for French waistcoats are based on Baudis 2008.

7. Arizzoli-Clémentel 1996, pp.50–51; V&A: *Suite de Nouveaux Cahiers de Vestes et de Gilets à la mode formant la 5eme Suite de l'Oeuvre de Ranson* (Paris 1780); V&A: E.1368-73–1906. E.1372–1906 is close to gilet T.212–1972.

8. '… de passe sur les coutures – veste en plain, garnie de ses quilles, la somme de 2000 [*livres*], en argent à un tiers de diminution' (inscription partly erased).

9. Riello 2006, p.xvii. Clothes of a wage-earner might be worth nearly 800 *livres* in contrast to 62,000 *livres* for the nobility at the beginning of the eighteenth century. Roche 1994, table 4, p.94. Riello, G., *A Foot in the Past. Consumers, Producers and Footwear in the Long Eighteenth Century* (Oxford, 2006).

10. '… boutons larges commes des écus de six livres'. G. Touchard-Lafosse quoted in Laing 2006, p.88. The buttonholes on the design are 0.9 × W.3.4 cm.

11. Delpierre 1983, p.185.

12. Baudis 2008, p.85.

13. There is also a *gilet* embroidered with macaques, made 1780–90. V&A: T.49–1948. Hart and North 1998, p.108. The design is in the Musée des Tissus: MT: A/334.35. The macaques are close to 'Le Papion' and 'L'Ouandérou' in 'Histoire Naturelle', Diderot, D., *Dictionnaire des Sciences …* tome VI, *Recueil de Planches* (Paris 1768), figs 1 and 2.

14. Baudis 2008, p.113.

15. Jaenen 1973, p.15.

16. Baudis 2008, p.113 and NMI: 238-1902 analysed pp.104–129, pl.2.65. See Ribeiro 1988, p.42, concerning the fashion for *élégants* who were prepared to wear dress that defied convention.

17. Rothstein 1984, p.31–2. Ribeiro and Cumming 1989, p.231.

18. Rothstein 1984, p.32.

19. Thunder 2006.

20. Morning visiting dress, 1827, hand-coloured print, 1827, V&A: E.1601–1968.

21. Higgin 1885, pp.20–21.

22. Buck 1984, pp.172, 174.

23. Leymarie, Jean, *Chanel* (New York, 1987), pp.82–4.

24. Royal Scottish Museum 1965, p.7.

25. Pritchard, accessed 2011, http://en.wikipedia.org/wiki/Mary Kessell/accessed 21 June 2011.

26. Royal Scottish Museum 1965, p.10.

27. Aberdeen City Arts Department 1989, pp.4, 17.

28. Rew, C. 'Foreword', Aberdeen City Arts Department, 1989, n.p

29. Aberdeen City Arts Department 1989, p.11; Couture beading 2010 http//www.couturebeading.com/aboutus.html, accessed 25 June 2012.

30. Flett 1990.

31. Catherine Woram updated by Owen James, 'Workers for Freedom' http://www.answers.com/topic/workers-for-freedom, accessed 25 April 2012. Garments with appliqué embroidery were modelled in a series of WFF trade cards held in the PDP Collection. V&A: E.35-6–1986; E.38-9–1986.

Accessories

1. Guilmard 1880–81, pp.87–9.

2. V&A: E.845-9–1939.

3. For images of horse trappings, see Scheuer 1983, p.104.

4. Margaretha Helm, *Kunst-und Fleiss-übende Nadel-Ergötzungen oder neu-erfundenes Neh-und Stick-Buch / The Delights of the Art and Industry of the Practizing Needle or the Newly-Invented Sewing and Embroidery Book* (Nuremberg, *c*.1725 and *c*.1742) Thunder 2010, pp.409–27.

5. 'Das Meister Stuck hat gemacht LvdKoch'.

6. Marshall 2008, pp.62, 227. Helm, *The Delights* (see note 4); Margaretha Helm, *Continuatio der Kunst–und Fleiss-übenden Nadel-Ergötzung oder des neu-ersonnenen Besondern Nehe–Buchs, dritter Theil / Continuation of the Delights of the Art and Industry of the Practizing Needle or the Newly-Invented Special Sewing Book Third Part* (Nuremberg, *c*.1725); Thunder 2010; V&A: L.1443–1982; E.3386-7–1931; E.5062–1905.

7. Margaretha Helm, *Fortgesetzter Kunst-und Fleiss-übender Nadel-auch Laden-Gewirck-Ergötzungen oder des neu-erfundenen Neh und Stick Buchs Anderer Theil / Further Delights of the Art and Industry of the Practizing Needle and Loom or the Newly-Invented Sewing and Embroidery Book Another Part* (Nuremberg, *c*.1742) Thunder 2010.

8. Adhémar 1849, p.432; V&A: E.4318-64–1910.

9. Ribeiro and Cumming 1989, p.231.

10. Cumming 1998, p.47.

11. Embroidery design for a clock from a volume of designs by Anna Margaretha Hertzog (worked about 1774), Nuremberg, V&A: E.1277–1923; designs for embroidered clocks from an eighteenth-century volume, V&A: 25689.8–9; Christoph Weigel, *New Neues Neh und Strickbuch / Needle and Knitting Book*, (Nuremberg 1784): V&A: 25637.

12. Seventeenth-century Italian or Spanish stockings with identical embroidered clocks are in the Museum of Fine Arts, Boston: inv.43.1941.a-b.

13. V&A: E.3402–1932; E.5090–1905; E.1152–1932.

14. V&A: D.1033–1901; D.1035–1901 and D.1041–1901.

15. 'Bretelles pour broder sur canvas de soie'.

16. Buck 1984, pp.24–5.

17. Jackson 2002, pp.168–71. Collars by Jessie Newbery that are similar to the Liberty's collar design are V&A: Circ.189–1953; T.65–1953.

18. Cumming 1998, p.29.

19. V&A: E.5066–1905.

20. Johann Georg Merz, 'Ein Frauenzimmer im Winter ausgehend' ('A young woman going out in winter').

21. Holme 1688, bk II, Chaps.XIX, fol. 469, no.126, and CXXIV, p.482.

22. V&A: T.205-12–1968.

23. V&A: D.1038–1901. The matching motifs for the sides (not illustrated) are on the same sheet of designs.

Furnishings

1. Clabburn 1988, pp.99–100.

2. Georges Charmeton, *Plusieurs Sortes d'Ornements, comme Panneaux ou Montans, Scabellons, Plafonds, Pantes de lits Servants à la Broderie / All sorts of Ornament, such as Panels, Pedestals, Uprights, Ceilings, Pantes for Beds suitable for Embroidery* (Paris, *c*.1660). Guilmard 1880–81, pp.67–8; Berlin 1939, p.51.

3. Thunder 2010.

4. Ripa, *Cesare, Della Piu Che Novissima Iconologia* […] (Padua, 1630), p.595.

5. Evidence of brides embroidering is contained in information received from Dr Bock in 1883 recorded in registered entry for napkin of 1620–50 purchased from the Bock collection, V&A: 8691–1863.

6. Margaretha Helm, *Continuation der Kunst-und Fleiss-übenden Nadel-Ergötzung oder des neu-ersonnenen besondern Nehe-Buchs, dritter Theil / Continuation of the Delights of the Art and Industry of the Practizing Needle or the Newly-Invented Special Sewing Book Third Part* (Nuremberg, *c*.1725).

7. British Library, Add. MS 5751, cited in Thurley 2003, p.416, and Murdoch 2008, p.4.

8. Reattribution by Murdoch 2008, p.4.

9. The connection between Daniel Marot and the embroidered hangings was first discovered by Coutts 1988; the record drawing and the two design drawings are V&A: 8480.7; 8480.12; 8480.14.

10. Coutts 1988.

11. Jackson-Stops 1980; Murdoch 1985, p.188; Murdoch 2008, p.3; Montagu House was demolished in 1845–52 to build the British Museum (1823–47) by Sir Robert Smirke. Two record drawings of painted panels from Montagu House: V&A: 8480.6-7.

12. V&A: 8480.14.

13. Embroidered hangings pl.128: putto at base: RCIN 28228.5; pl.130: bust at top: RCIN 28228.1.

14. Coutts 1988.

15. Sebastian Edwards, Deputy Chief Curator and Head of Collections, Historic Royal Palaces, pers. comm. from 22 March 2012.

16. Murdoch 2008, p.4; Sebastian Edwards, pers. comm. from 22 March 2012.

17. Levey 1988, p.8.

18. Marsh 2008, p.30.

19. Morris 1982, p.20.

20. Simpkin and Marshall 1854; Wooster 1866–7, p.422.

21. Heather Porter, Senior Upholstery Conservator, V&A. Measurements of the roses: 10 × W.9.5 cm

22. Harvey and Press 1991, p.122; Parry 1993, pp.20–21

23. V&A: AAD/1990/6/file 3; Calloway and Orr 2011, p.264; Parry 1983, pp.21, 145.

24. Parry 2005, pp.115–6; Harvey 1991, p.176, 254.

25. V&A: Circ.300–1960.

26. Morris & Co. Catalogue, *Embroidery Work* (London 1913), n.p.

27. Harvey 1991, p.168.

28. May Morris, *Decorative Needlework* (London 1893), quoted in William Morris Gallery 1989, p.1.

29. Ibid.

30. Jackson 2002, p.158; Parry 1996, pp.57–68; William Morris Gallery 1989, p.1.

31. V&A: E.27-31–1940 and E.35-36–1940 & E.960–1940.

32. William Morris Gallery 1989, p.2.

33. 'L'Amor che muove il sole e l'altre stele'.

34. Christian 1975, p.72.

35. Ajmar-Wollheim and Dennis 2006, pp.112–13, pl.7.10; pp.152–63, pl.11.13; pp.342–51, pls 24.5 and 24.7.

36. Margaretha Helm, *Kunst-und Fleiss-übende Nadel-Ergötzungen oder neu-erfundenes Neh-und Stick-Buch / The Delights of the Art and Industry of the Practizing Needle or the Newly-Invented Sewing and Embroidery Book* (Nuremberg *c*.1725 and *c*.1742); Thunder 2010.

37. The second design is a supplement to *Modes et Travaux, Fashions and Works* no.719, (November 1960); V&A: E.1352–1986.

38. Beck 1995, p.137.

39. Turner 1996, p.17. Turner, Jane, (ed.), *The Dictionary of Art*, (London 1996), vol.30.

40. V&A: T.1–1959.

Plate 153
Bord for furnishing
Lyon, *c.*1785
Bodycolour, 24 x 22.7 cm
V&A: E.227–1930

Glossary

appliqué
A decorative technique in which a shaped piece of fabric or other material is attached to a ground fabric to form a pattern.

blackwork
Embroidery using only black threads.

bobbin lace
Lace made by plaiting or twisting together a number of threads around pins that control the design. The threads are wound on small bobbins and the work is supported on a pillow.

bord
A presentation design to be shown to a client.

brocade
This term had a precise technical meaning in the seventeenth and eighteenth centuries indicating that design effects in a woven textile had been produced with an extra weft whose incorporation was limited to the width of the design produced.

broderie en rapport
Embroidery made from separate pieces joined together.

canetille
Metal embroidery thread covered in twisted or coiled gold wire, or made from heavy gold wire, either wavy or spiral, flattened by a roller.

chain stitch
Embroidery stitch forming interlocking flat chains.

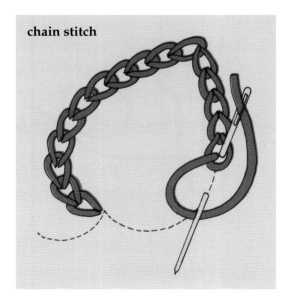

chain stitch

chenille
Tufted thread, usually of silk, which when worked creates a soft pile (from French word for caterpillar).

couching
Technique for securing a thread to the surface of a fabric by passing a finer thread in small stitches up from the back of the fabric to secure it; used when the decorative thread is too thick to pass through to the back of the fabric, or particularly precious or fragile (e.g. metal thread, *chenille*).

counted thread
Embroidery in which stitches are worked evenly by counting the number of threads of ground fabric over which the needle is taken.

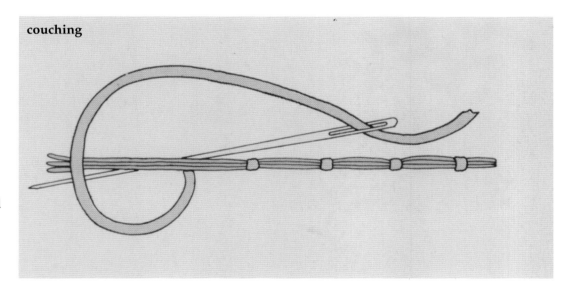

couching

coupon
Tracing of one complete repeat of a design, usually seven or eight inches long. These repeats were joined to complete a border.

crewel
Lightly twisted two-ply worsted (wool) yarn used in embroidery. Such embroidery is described as **crewel work**.

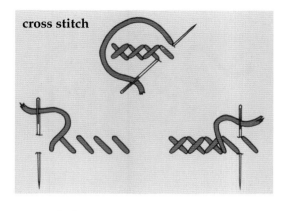

cross stitch

cross stitch
Embroidery on an evenly woven fabric in which each stitch, in the shape of a cross, may be completed before moving on to the next. Alternatively, it may be worked in two journeys, a row of diagonal stitches being made first, the needle then returning to the starting point making a row of opposing diagonals to complete the crosses.

cutwork
Originally an **appliqué** decoration of cut-out shapes, the name was then used to describe embroidery in which parts of the ground were cut away. From the mid-sixteenth century it was also the generic name for all forms of needle lace based on a woven ground.

damask
Patterned woven textile with one warp and one weft. The design is formed by the contrast of the binding systems, and appears on the face and back in reversed positions.

double running stitch
Running stitch worked in two journeys over the same line, with the stitch and space usually being of equal length; on the return journey the needle fills the spaces. Double running stitch creates an identical pattern on both sides of the fabric.

drawn thread work
Technique in which some threads are drawn out from the ground and remaining threads reinforced with stitches to create a decorative effect.

feather stitch
Embroidery stitch resembling branched coral or feathers.

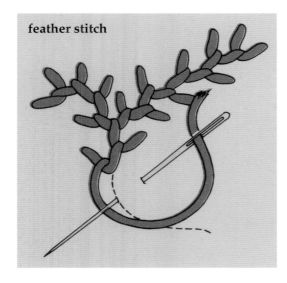

filé
Silver or silver-gilt strip wound on a silk or linen core.

free-machine embroidery
Also described as 'drawing with the needle', delineates stitched patterns, sometimes using a darning foot to hold the fabric down. The feed (or teeth) are lowered, so the work has to be guided by hand rather than being advanced by the grip of the teeth.

French knot
The needle is brought through where the knot is required. Thread is twisted round the needle several times, and the needle is returned and inserted close to where it was brought out, to create a small knot.

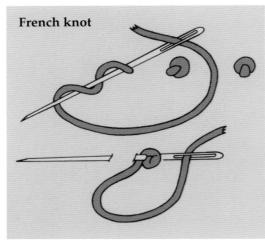

frisé
Metal thread made from silver or silver-gilt strip on a core, one end of which is twisted more tightly than the other, giving a crinkled effect.

gaufrure
Embroidery in the pattern of a waffle or wickerwork.

lacis
Handmade knotted net decorated with embroidery.

lawn
Fine, plain-weave linen or cotton with a silky finish, historically made in Laon, France.

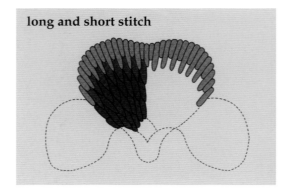

needle painting
Reproducing the effect of painting with embroidery stitches.

open Cretan stitch
A light, zigzag line of stitching suitable for a straight row or gentle curve.

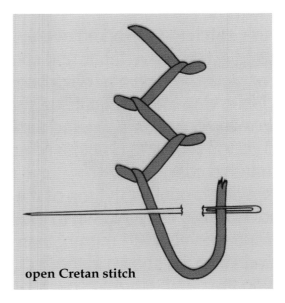

plaited knot stitch
Translated from the German *Zopffnot*, a braid stitch that needs a stiff thread to be most effective.

plush stitch
This stitch is made from a row of cross stitch over which is placed a narrow strip of card, secured by layered rows of close herringbone stitch. These are then cut along the strip of card to form a pile.

raised work
Embroidery worked in relief to create a three-dimensional effect.

running stitch
The simplest of all stitches, with the needle passing in and out of the fabric at regular intervals, picking up only one or two threads between each stitch.

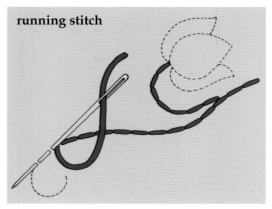

sampler
Piece of fabric on which different patterns and stitches have been worked for reference or as a demonstration of skill.

satin stitch
Close and regular stitches made by carrying the thread across the space to be filled and returning underneath the fabric to the starting point.

strapwork
Style of ornament composed of interlaced bands.

tent stitch
One of the most widely used counted thread stitches, worked on canvas in diagonal or horizontal rows.

twill
A type of weave creating rows of parallel diagonal lines.

whitework
Embroidery worked with white thread on a white ground.

worsted
Yarn or fabric made from combed long-staple wool.

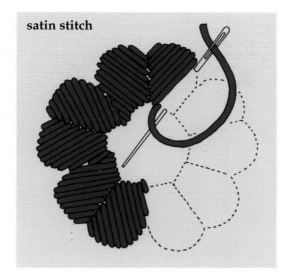

satin stitch

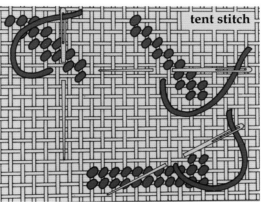

tent stitch

The diagrams and some explanations in this Glossary are based on the work of Mary Thomas, Dictionary of Embroidery Stitches, *new edition by Jan Eaton (Hodder & Stoughton, London, 1989). Some explanations are also based on Browne and Wearden (2003), pp.136–43, Marsh (2006 and 2008) and Baudis (2008).*

Bibliography

Aberdeen City Arts Department, *Bill Gibb: A Tribute to the Fashion Designer of the '70s* (Aberdeen 1989)

Adhémar, J., *Inventaire du Fonds Français après 1800* (Paris 1849)

Ajmar-Wollheim, M. and F. Dennis, *At Home in Renaissance Italy*, exh. cat., Victoria and Albert Museum, London (London 2006)

Arber, E. (ed), *A Transcript of the Registers of the Company of Stationers of London, 1554–1640*, vol.4 (London 1877)

Arrizoli-Clémental, P., 'Gilets brodes au XVIIIe siècle, *L'Oeil Magazine International d'Art*, no.478 (January 1996), pp.48–51

Arthur, L., *Embroidery 1600–1700 at the Burrell Collection* (London 1995)

Barker, N., *Two East Anglian Picture Books: A Facsimile of the Helmingham Herbal and Bestiary and Bodleian MS. Ashmole 1504* (London 1988)

Barker, N., *The Great Book of Thomas Trevilian: A facsimile manuscript in the Wormsley Library* (London 2000)

Baudis, M.G., 'Embroidery for Male Suiting in Lyon, 1780–1789: A Cultural Biography of the Designs in the National Museum of Ireland Collection Presented by J.H. Fitzhenry', unpublished Ph.D. thesis, National College of Art and Design, Dublin 2008

Beck, T., *The Embroiderer's Story: Needlework from the Renaissance to the Present Day* (Newton Abbot 1995)

Berlin, *Katalog der Ornamentstichsammlung der Staatlichen Kunstbibliothek* (Berlin 1939)

Blazy, G. et al., *The Textile Museum, Lyons: Guide to the Collections* (Lyon 2001)

Bradstock, P., *Painted with Thread: The Art of American Embroidery*, exh. cat. (Salem, MA, 2000)

Brooke, X., *The Lady Lever Art Gallery Catalogue of Embroideries* (Stroud 1992)

Brooks, M.M., *English Embroideries of the Sixteenth and Seventeenth Centuries in the Collection of the Ashmolean Museum* (Oxford 2004)

Browne, C. and J. Wearden, Jennifer, *Samplers from the Victoria and Albert Museum* (London 2003)

Buck, A., *Victorian Costume and Costume Accessories* (Bedford 1984)

Burman, B. (ed.), *The Culture of Sewing: Gender, Consumption and Home Dressmaking* (Oxford 1999)

Burman, B. et al., 'A history of pockets', http://www.vam.ac.uk/content/articles/a/history-of-pockets/)

Calloway, S., and L. Federle Orr (eds), *The Cult of Beauty: The Aesthetic Movement 1860–1900*, exh. cat., Victoria and Albert Museum, London (London 2011)

Christian, J., *The Paintings, Graphic and Decorative Work of Sir Edward Burne-Jones 1833–98*, exh. cat., Hayward Gallery, London (London 1975)

Clabburn, P., *The National Trust Book of Furnishing Textiles* (London 1988)

Clark, J. and A. Phillips, *The Concise Dictionary of Dress* (London 2010)

Coutts, H., 'Hangings for a Royal Closet', *Country Life* (13 October 1988), vol. 182, pp.232–3

Crawford, A., 'Crane, Walter (1845–1915)', *Oxford Dictionary of National Biography* (Oxford 2004); online edn http://www.oxforddnb.com/view/article/32616?docPos=1

Cumming, V., *The Visual History of Costume Accessories* (London 1998)

Cumming, E.S., 'Traquair [neé Moss], Phoebe Anna (1852–1936)' *Oxford Dictionary of National Biography* (Oxford 2004); online edn http://www.oxforddnb.com/view/article/38949

Delpierre, M., *Broderies Françaises au Musée de la Mode et du Costume de la Ville de Paris* (Tokyo 1983)

Doppelmayr, G., *Historische Nachricht von den Nürnbergischen Mathematicis und Künstlerin* (Nuremberg 1730)

Flett, K., 'Fashion Review', *The Sunday Times Magazine* (2 September 1990), pp.69–71

Foster, V., *A Visual History of Costume: The Nineteenth Century* (New York 1984)

Gascoigne, B., *How to Identify Prints: A complete guide to manual and mechanical processes from woodcut to ink-jet* (London 1986)

Gordon-Smith, M., *Pillement* (Cracow 2006)

Guilmard, D., *Les Maîtres Ornemanistes* (Paris 1880–81)

Hackney, F., 'Use Your Hands for Happiness': Home Craft and Make-do-and-Mend in British Women's Magazines in the 1920s and 1930s', *Journal of Design History*, vol.19, no.1 (2006), pp.23–38

Harrison, Harrod & Co.'s Postal Directory and Gazetteer of Devonshire and Cornwall (London 1862)

Hart, A. and S. North, Historical Fashion in Detail: The 17th and 18th Centuries (London 1985)

Harvey, C. and J. Press, *Design and Enterprise in Victorian Britain* (Manchester 1991)

Higgin, L., *Art as Applied to Dress* (London 1885)

Holme, R., *The Academy of Armory* (Chester 1688)

Hulse, L., *Royal School of Needlework Handbook of Embroidery by Laetitia Higgin (1880)* (East Molesey 2000)

Jackson, A., *The V&A Guide to Period Styles* (London 2002)

Jackson-Stops, G., 'Daniel Marot and the 1st Duke of Montagu', *Nederlands Kunsthistorisch Jaarboek*, vol.31 (1980), pp.244–62

Jaenen, C., *Aspects of French-Amerindian Cultural Contact in the Sixteenth and Seventeenth Centuries* (Ontario 1973)

Keene, J., *The Bath Directory* (Bath 1826)

Kelly, E.R. *Post Office Directory of Devonshire and Cornwall* (London 1856)

Kelly, E.R. *The Post Office Directory of Devonshire* (London 1866, 1883, 1889, 1893, 1897)

King, D. and S. Levey, *The Victoria and Albert Museum's Textile Collection*, vol.3: *Embroidery in Britain from 1200 to 1750* (London 1993)

Laing, A., et al., *Catalogue of Drawings for Architecture, Design and Ornament: The James A. De Rothschild Bequest at Waddesdon Manor* (Aylesbury 2006)

Lambert, S., *Pattern and Design: Designs for the Decorative Arts 1480–1980* (London 1983)

Lemire, B., *Dress, Culture and Commerce: The English Clothing Trade before the Factory* (London 1997)

Levey, S., *Lace: A History* (Leeds 1983)

Levey, S., *Discovering Embroidery of the 19th century* (Aylesbury 1989)

Levey, S., *An Elizabethan Inheritance: The Hardwick Hall Textiles* (Swindon 1998)

Levey, S., 'The Background to Shorleyker's Book', *A Schole-house for the Needle: Produced from the original book printed in 1632 and now in the private collection of John and Elizabeth Mason* (Much Wenlock, Shropshire, 1998)

Levey, S., *The Embroideries at Hardwick Hall: A Catalogue* (Swindon 2007)

Lomas, Elizabeth, *Guide to the Archive of Art and Design* (London 2001)'

Lotz, A., *Bibliographie der Modelbücher* (Leipzig 1933)

Marsh, G., *18th Century Embroidery Techniques* (Lewes 2006)

Marsh, G., *19th Century Embroidery Techniques* (Lewes 2008)

Marshall, Noreen, *Dictionary of Children's Clothes: 1700s to Present* (London 2008), pp.62 & 227

Miller, L.E., 'Meeting the Needs of Manufacturers: The Education of Silk Designers in Eighteenth century Lyon', *Proceedings of the Textile Society of America* (1998), pp.272–81

Morrall, A. and M. Watt, *English Embroidery from the Metropolitan Museum of Art, 1580–1700: Twixt Art and Nature* (New York 2008)

Morris, Barbara, *Victorian Embroidery* (London 1982)

Morris & Co.'s, Commercial Directory and Gazetteer of Devonshire (Notts 1870)

Murdoch, T., *The Quiet Conquest: The Huguenots 1685–1985*, exh. cat., Museum of London (London 1985)

Murdoch, Tessa, 'Marot, Daniel (1661–1752) Oxford Dictionary of National Biography, Oxford University Press, 2004; online edn, Jan 2008 http://www.oxforddnb.com/view/article/39328, accessed 18 July 2012

Nevinson, J.L., 'Peter Stent and John Overton, publishers of Embroidery Designs', *Apollo*, vol. 24 (November 1936), pp.279–83

Nevinson, J.L., *Catalogue of English Domestic Embroidery of the Sixteenth and Seventeenth Centuries* (London 1950)

Nevinson, J.L., 'The Embroidery Patterns of Thomas Trevelyon', *The Walpole Society*, vol. 61 (1968), pp.1–38

Nevinson, J.L., 'John Nelham, Embroiderer', *The Bulletin of the Needle and Bobbin Club* vol.65, nos 1 and 2 (1982), pp.17–19

Paganino, A., *Libro primo [-quarto] de rechami p[er] elquale se impara in diversi modi lordine e il modo de recamare ...* (Venice 1878–80)

Paine, S., *Embroidered Textiles: Traditional Patterns from Five Continents* (London 2008)

Palliser, Mrs B., *History of Lace* (London 1902)

Parker, R., *The Subversive Stitch: Embroidery and the Making of the Feminine* (London 1984)

Parry, L., *William Morris Textiles* (London 1983)

Parry, L., *Textiles of the Arts and Crafts Movement* (London 2005)

Parry, Linda, 'May Morris, embroidery and Kelmscott', William *Morris. Art &*

Kelmscott (London, 1996), pp.57–68

Privat-Savigny, M-A., Musée *des Tissus de Lyon. Collection Guide* (Lyon, 2010).

Ribeiro, A., *Fashion in the French Revolution* (London 1988)

Ribeiro, A. and V. Cumming, *The Visual History of Costume* (London 1989)

Riello, G., *A Foot in the Past: Consumers, Producers and Footwear in the Long Eighteenth Century* (Oxford 2006)

Roche, D., *The Culture of Clothing: Dress and Fashion in the Ancien Régime* (Cambridge 1994)

Rothstein, N., *Silk Designs of the Eighteenth Century in the Collection of the Victoria and Albert Museum* (London 1990)

Rothstein, N. et al., *Four Hundred Years of Fashion* (London 1984)

Royal Scottish Museum, *Catalogues of Embroideries given to the Museum by the Needlework Development Scheme* (Edinburgh 1965)

Saint-Aubin, C.G. de, *L'Art du Brodeur* (Paris 1770)

Saunders, G., *Picturing Plants: An Analytical History of Botanical Illustration* (London 1995)

Scheuer, N. (trans.) and E. Maeder, *Art of the Embroiderer by Charles Germain de Saint-Aubin Designer to the King 1770* (Los Angeles 1983)

Simpkin and Marshall, *A Directory City and Borough of Bath ...* (Bath 1854)

Smith & Co., *Bath and Somerset Directory* (1865–6)

Thomas, M., *Dictionary of Embroidery Stitches* (London 1934)

Thornton, P., *Baroque and Rococo Silks* (London 1965)

Thunder, M., 'Designs and Clients for Embroidered Dress 1782–94', *Textile History* vol.37, no.1 (May 2006), pp.82–90

Thunder, M., 'Deserving Attention: Magaretha Helm's Designs for Embroidery in the Eighteenth Century', *Journal of Design History*, vol.23, no.4 (2010), pp.409–27

Thurley, S., *Hampton Court: A Social and Architectural History* (Yale 2003)

Tomlinson, M., *Three Generations in the Honiton Lace Trade: A Family History* (Exeter 1983)

Toomer, H., *Embroidered with white: The 18th century fashion for Dresden lace and other whiteworked accessories* (2008)

White, W., *History, Gazetteer and Directory of the County of Devon* (Sheffield 1890)

White, W. History, *Gazetteer and Directory*

of the County of Devon (Sheffield 1878–9)

William Morris Gallery, *May Morris 1862–1938* (London 1989)

Wooster, W., *The Post-Office Directory* (Bath 1864–7)

Acknowledgements

Many thanks are due to Mark Eastment, Lesley Ellis Miller, Anjali Bulley, and the V&A's Publications Advisory Committee for supporting this publication proposal. I am very grateful to Julius Bryant, Chris Breward, Elizabeth Miller, and Glenn Adamson for authorizing periods in Research Department and for research grants. Particular thanks are due to Elizabeth Miller for her support for this book, overseeing the selection of material for photography, and for her comments as the first reader. Special thanks are due to readers, Clare Browne and to Christopher Marsden, for their challenging and helpful comments. Special thanks are due to Christopher Wilk, and Furniture, Textiles and Fashion Department, and particularly Suzanne Smith for providing access to the Collection. I should like to thank Frances Hartog, Textiles Conservation, for conservation of dress and textiles for photography and to Sara Hodges for her proactive approach in this and her photography. Thanks are also due to Roisin Inglesby, Sally Williams, Frances Willis, Matthew Storey, and Kaitlyn Whitley for organising photography. Thank you to Oriole Cullen for her advice in dress mounting and to Matt Greer for his work. I should like to thank the following for help with research: Bryony Bartlett-Rawlings, Macushla Baudis, Theodor Böll, Clare Browne, Victoria Button, Alan Derbyshire, Edwina Ehrman, Sarah Grant, Sarah Lister, Noreen Marshall, Pietro Menis, MaryAnn Meredith, Daniel Milford-Cottam, Laura Miller, Harry Pilkington, Nick Smith, Michael Snodin, Matthew Storey, James Sutton, Rosie Taylor-Davies, Abraham Thomas, Evelin Wetter, Eva White, Gareth Williams, Esmé Whittaker and Louise Wood.

I am very grateful to Elizabeth and John Mason for allowing me to study their pattern book and to Linda O'Reilly and Nic Harris, Kangol Headwear Ltd. I am especially grateful to staff from Historic Royal Palaces: Gabriella Barbieri, Brett Dolman, Sebastian Edwards, and Laurie Gibbs.